The Folklore of the British Isles
General Editor: Venetia J. Newall

The Folklore of
The Lake District

In memory of my parents and forbears
Thextons and Aireys
of
Lunesdale and Kentdale

The Folklore
of
The Lake District

MARJORIE ROWLING

Drawings by Terence Dalley

ROWMAN AND LITTLE FIELD
Totowa, New Jersey

First published in the United States 1976
by ROWMAN AND LITTLEFIELD, Totowa, N.J.
© Marjorie Rowling 1976

ISBN 0–87471–839–2

Printed in Great Britain

Contents

Acknowledgments

The author particularly wishes to thank Mr J. J. Bagley, Reader in History at the University of Liverpool, Dr N. B. Lewis, Emeritus Professor of Medieval History at the University of Sheffield and Mrs. Venetia Newall of the University of London and Honorary Secretary of the Folklore Society, who have so generously read and helpfully criticized the book in typescript. She is most grateful also to Professor Kenneth Jackson of the Department of Celtic in the University of Edinburgh for so fully answering queries on early Cumbrian history and sources, and to the Librarians and Staffs of the Cumbria County Library, Carlisle, of the Ambleside, Kendal and Windermere Public Libraries, as to those of the London Library who have made books and photostats available. Also sincere thanks are due to the many Cumbrians who have given valuable information on the lore of their districts.

Foreword

North-western England is notable for the great amount of obvious and visible history still to be found: Roman remains, castles from the unsettled border past, workings connected with industrial development and, of course, monuments to the tourist trade. After the railway was completed in 1847, the tiny hamlet of Birthwaite grew into modern Windermere, a thriving holiday centre near the former junction of the three Lakeland counties. Where the M6 now sweeps north, between Kendal and Kirkby Stephen, an English officer campaigning against the Scots a century earlier (1745), wrote of his journey between the two towns: 'We frequently come to valleys, which with great fear and danger we descend, they being very steep. This was the most strange journey I ever made.'

Twenty years ago, John Armthwaite, a contributor to *Cumbria,* noticed how the reactions of visitors had changed. 'There was a time when travellers looked at our Lakeland fells and shuddered. Words like "awesome" and "dreadful" crept into their writing. Not to-day.' The environment had become familiar, not only through increased accessibility and greater uniformity, but because of literacy and the modern spread of information. The writer of 1745 was of course literate, and yet he was amazed by the local rivers, which were 'quite different from those in the Southern parts of England'.

In *Enjoying the Lakes,* the author Edmund Hodge mentions two distinct attitudes towards the area. 'There is one arising from the countryman's intimate knowledge, and the other springing from the personal discovery, often nostalgic in feeling, of the townsman. It is the latter group which starts with the advantages, frequently carrying the heavier armament of professional talent, or a sharper spearhead of feeling; but when there is not something like this to rely on, this group includes by far the worst.' Folklorists may well consider the comment, which underlines on the one hand a tendency to fossilise the social environment, so often practised by well-intentioned regional patriots; and on the other, the homesickness for an illusory past, which gives the most trivial cultural residues an apparent aura of virtue, concealing their real significance. The task of the folklorist is neither to idealise, nor to perpetuate the past. His job is to record the events which are his concern, including the present, to analyse them as an aspect of man's ideological view of life, and to place them in historical perspective.

Eight years after Windermere became accessible by railway, Harriet Martineau published her *Guide to the Lakes*. It is a pleasant, useful little book, but very much the product of a generation convinced by man's supposed ascendency over nature, and its by-product, a reformed humanity. Welcoming technical progress in the textile industry, she did not view it as a social challenge to the declining Lakeland weavers. On the contrary, the process must continue until 'the primitive population, having lost its safety of isolation and independence, shall have given place to a new set of inhabitants.'

In fact, Miss Martineau was an intelligent, progressive author, altogether different from the agricultural commentator, Arthur Young, writing of the fenland just before her own birth in Norfolk: ' . . . so wild a place nurses up a race of people as wild as the fens'. This attitude persists, though modern knowledge can place it in perspective. Edward Storey, a recent writer on the same area and himself a fenman, comments: 'Our geographical environment influences us as much as our real environment. Places have their own spirit and character. We take, absorb, interpret and give back' — and, as the folklorist knows, the interchanging pattern goes on and on. The context may vary, but the content does not.

Wordsworth and his friends were also concerned with the influence of man's surroundings. One day in 1797 he was with Coleridge and the political reformer John Thelwall in the Quantocks, having treasonable thoughts. They came to a beauty spot, and Coleridge ponderously began: 'Citizen John, this is a fine place to talk treason in.' 'Nay, Citizen Samuel,' was the answer, 'it is rather a place to make a man forget that there is any necessity for treason.' This remark reminds us of the argument about folklore's proper milieu: is it to be sought in an urban or rural setting? But the debate is unimportant, since it only arises when form, not content, is thought relevant. Of course social conditions cannot be considered apart from their environment, and the natural locale can become almost inseparable. Just as with an understanding of political or historical events, it is in illustrating fundamental aspects of the society in which it occurs that the value of folklore lies. Why, for instance, was Pace Egging practised around Langdale about a century ago? A correspondent of the Folklore Survey shows that the main reason was necessity. 'Parents, often very poor, rigged their kiddies up to collect their own Peace Eggs this way. The modern child knows nothing of this sort of thing . . . some of the boys who came Peace Egging that day were [later] killed in the quarries about here, but Little Lord Nelson [then about 8] is still living and over 80 years.' Why does Pace Egging survive in some districts? Either, I would guess, because of antiquarianism, or since it is felt to encourage a healthy community spirit.

Marjorie Rowling is a native of Westmorland. After graduating in history at Manchester University, she became a teacher and, following her marriage, settled in Kendal. A life-long devotee of the Lake District and its traditions, she is the author of two novels largely based on that area. She also contributed two books to the *Everyday Life* series, *Everyday Life in Medieval Times* and *Everyday Life of Medieval Travellers.* She is now a Vice-President of the Cumbrian Literary Group and, apart from her lifelong association with the Lake District, brings to the present series her own special interests. The result is an excellent book, illustrating the manner in which varying disciplines have bearing on our subject.

London University   Venetia Newall
February 1976

CUMBRIA

IRISH SEA

SEA

SOLWAY FIRTH

Moricambe Bay

Nith

Criffel

Liddel Water

Liddel Strength
Carwinley Mill
Netherby
Longtown
Arthuret
Bewcastle

Irthing

Birdoswald
Triermain Cas.
Lanercost Priory
Upper Denton
Nether Denton
Scaleby
Irthington
Brampton
St Martin's

Esk
Rockcliffe Marsh
Bowness
Anthorn
Grinsdale

Wetheral Abbey
Constantine's Cells
Carlisle

Eden

Silloth
Abbey Town
Bromfield
Wigton
Old Carlisle
Wolsty Castle (site of)
Holm St Cuthbert

High Hesket
Haresceugh Cas.
Alston
Fiends Fell

Aspatria
Bothel
Bolton Old Ch.
Caldbeck
Caldew
Tarn Wadling
Addingham Ch.
Kirkoswald
Castle Sowerby
Glassonby
Melmerby
Gt. Salkeld
Long Meg
Langwathby
Skirwith

Maryport
Dearham
Isel
Derwent
Bassenthwaite Lake
Skiddaw
Bowscale Tarn
Mungrisdale
Greystoke
Edenhall
Penrith
Eamont
Brougham Cas.
Mayborough
Round Table
Temple Sowerby
Kirkby Thore

Workington
Cockermouth
Blencathra
Threlkeld
Julian Bower
Cliburn
Appleby

Distington
Ullock
Mockerkin Tarn
Loweswater
Crosthwaite
Keswick
Vale of St John
Derwentwater
Ullswater
Lyvennet
Hoff
Eden
Brou

Lamplugh
Crummock Water
Buttermere
Borrowdale
Thirlmere
Martindale
Bampton
Crosby Ravensworth
Warcop
Musgrave
Crosby Garre

St Bees Head
Whitehaven
St Bees
Ennerdale Water
Egremont
Wasdale Head
Helvellyn
Dunmail Raise
Grisedale Tarn
Patterdale
Shap
British Settlements
Kirkby Stephen

Gosforth
Wastwater
Irt
Burnmoor
Boot
Esk
Eskdale
Birkby Fell
Grasmere
Rydal
Kirkstone Pass
Haweswater
Tebay
Ravenstonedale
Lammersi
Ca

Ravenglass
Muncaster Cas.
Ulpha
Dudden
Coniston
Esthwaite Water
Ambleside
Troutbeck
Belle I.
Windermere Town
Selside
Wild Boar Fell
Pe
dra
Cas

Sunken Kirk
Broughton
Satter-thwaite
Blawith
Newby Bridge
Finsthwaite
Bowness
Crook
Windermere
Kendal
Bleaze Hall
Killington
Sedbergh
Dent

Kirksanton
Millom
Kirkby Ireleth
Blawith
Winster
Witherslack
Ulpha
Levens Hall
Heversham
Kent
Bela
Beetham
Kirkby Lonsdale

Furness Abbey
Stainton
Walney Island
Barrow-in-Furness
Ulverston
Cartmel
Grange
Arnside
Humphrey Head
Burton in Kendale

MORECAMBE BAY

0   5   10 miles
0   8   16 km

Introduction

Geographical position and historical events have had a major influence on the folklore of Cumbria and the Lake District National Park contained within it. The Lake District has been defined as that area within Cumbria which comprises the central dome of mountains which, with its valleys, streams and rivers, also contains the major lakes and tarns of England. Since the wider area of the former Lake Counties of England – Westmorland, Cumberland and the Districts of Furness and Cartmel, North of the Sands – has always formed a geographical unity, enclosed as it is on three sides by natural boundaries, the Solway Firth, Irish Sea and Morecambe Bay, with the barrier of the Pennines to the east, the area has also possessed an overall cultural unity, though with regional differences. It is the folklore, legends and traditional ways of life of this wider area of Cumbria – the new name now given to the former Lake Counties – which is the subject of this book.

Cumbria faces north across the Solway to Galloway and west to the Isle of Man and Ireland. Since the sea, especially in the past, was a highway rather than a barrier, these localities have had a close cultural link with our district. On the stones of the Cumbrian prehistoric circles are found carvings of cups, concentric rings with radial channels, spirals and other motifs which are found in the Neolithic Passage Graves of the Boyne in Ireland as well as on stones in Scotland and Northumberland. The symbolism of these ancient patterns is without doubt an expression of the religion and folk beliefs of these early peoples. Their art was abstract and as Evan Hadingham has written:

> Surely it must also be symbolic of values too sacred or intricate to express by images of ordinary reality . . . The appearance of these designs not merely in Europe but all over the world among ancient traditions as widespread as those of Brazil, India, and Australia, indicates the fundamental nature of the impulse to create these simple abstract forms.

It was from Ireland, from north of the Solway and from Northumbria that the earliest Christian missionaries came to Cumbria, that is as far as written traditional records show. Christianity in turn produced its own magnificent religious and mythological symbols found carved on the stone crosses, fonts and tympanums of the district.

Roman rule appears to have made little impact on the ways of life of the British, in general. Nevertheless, some of the most interesting legends and traditions of Penrith and its district can be traced back, in part, to Roman influence, for even before the withdrawal of the Romans from Britain, modern scholars have shown that the imperial policy was to advance friendly native princes in north and north-west Britain as well as elsewhere, to a regal status; this north-western region became known as Rheged and is thought to have stretched from southern Galloway to the Lune, or even the Ribble in the south, and east to include Catraeth — modern Catterick, in Yorkshire. Its princes traced their descent from men with Roman names and as they were allies of Rome were regarded as wielding imperial power so that the adjective *Caesarius* was attached to them. King Urien and his son Owain of Rheged, whose administrative centre is now thought to have been Carlisle, became during the 6th and 7th centuries Christian champions of British resistance to the pagan Angles and were sung by their court bards as legendary heroes even during their lifetime. Later, these traditional stories merged with lore about Owain or Eugenius of Strathclyde and Cumbria who, during the tenth-century revival of British power in the north-west, also became a hero of resistance to the English. Hence the name of the local Penrith giant was Hugh or Owen Caesarius representing in traditional lore the folk memories of the days of Cymric greatness.

And what of King Arthur in the north-west? It has been said that there is little Arthurian lore in Cumbria. Nevertheless it can be clearly shown that place names, early British poems, medieval romances and the lore connected with ancient monuments have much to tell us about Arthur in the north-west. Indeed, there is documentary proof of Carlisle being regarded as Arthur's military centre in a charter of Henry I's reign (1100-35), for this document records a transfer of land which is stated to lie near to *Arthur's burh* in Carlisle. This building was probably Roman in origin, but *burh* is a Saxon word used to describe a fortified dwelling and, since it is used to define the position of land about 1100, the building must have been well known by that name before that date. Now Marie de France (Temp. Henry II) is thought to have been the first writer to place Arthur's court in Carlisle in her *lais* of *Lanval*. She has stated that she based her fables and lais on earlier songs of the Bretons, who may in turn have learned them from the Welsh. But the naming, before AD 1100, of an ancient building in Carlisle as *Arthur's burh* – a fact officially recorded by that date, but obviously in popular use before then – shows that a tradition already existed of the presence of that king's fortified residence as having been in the city before *Lanval* was written, and not – as is generally stated – that Marie de France originated the placing of Arthur's court in Carlisle. Chrétien de Troyes then seems to have adopted the same idea by following Marie's example and making Carlisle Arthur's centre in his romances also.

Much of the British folklore of Cumbria must have merged with that of the English, when the apparently peaceful Anglian influx from the east began during the seventh century. This seems to have followed the marriage of Oswy of Northumbria to Urien's great-granddaughter, Rieinmelth, Queen of the Lightning, around 650. The survival of many early British place names in Cumbria shows that the British were not exterminated but continued their own way of life on upland farms and settlements, while Anglians preferred the richer pastures of more lowland regions. Professor Jackson states that linguistic evidence points to the British having become bilingual and proficient in Anglo-Saxon. Also, that there was probably a considerable degree of intermarriage between Saxon and Briton. He concludes:

Britons lived on in numbers under their English overlords in Cumbria, especially in remote glens which are characteristic of parts of the area. The wild country on the Northumberland border shows a special survival of British place names. One scholar thinks that a British speaking population survived here until the 11th. century, but Jackson ascribes the place names to the 10th. century when the British of Strathclyde reconquered and reoccupied North Cumbria. The Britons out-numbered the English in Cumbria and lived on racially little affected by the invasion, remaining fundamentally Celtic. They kept their language longer than the outnumbered serfs of eastern England: thus their place-names had a better chance of survival.

These conclusions, also point to a likelihood of British legends and traditions surviving, so that the Arthurian lore reported about Ravenglass by Denton and Sandford — two local historians, in the seventeenth century, quoting a medieval chronicler — links up with the earlier lore about Arthur in Carlisle.

In recounting and discussing the folklore and legends of Cumbria the earliest written recording has been given where possible, together with later versions. By this method interesting and valuable deductions can often be drawn. In the story of Hugh Heard, the giant of Troutbeck, for instance, the earliest written version of around 1662 depicts him as a champion archer against the Scots, but a century later he is famed as an invincible wrestler, which gives a clue as to the period when wrestling was ousting archery as a popular sporting activity. The lore concerning Hugh also throws considerable light on local customs and character.

Finally, the chief aim of this book has been to try to gather into one volume as much as possible of the researches of modern scholars on the prehistoric Celtic and Arthurian lore, on the earliest texts, legends and medieval romances, Norse sagas and mythology and the study of place-names, which concern the region so attractive to those who love it, not only for its outstanding beauty but also for the evidences — still preserved and kept alive — of the folk who have created it from the time of the prehistoric circle builders, through the work of Celts and British, Angles, Irish-Norse, Bretons and Normans, down to those present-day Cumbrians and dalesfolk who, while retaining much from ancient traditions, continue to create the modern folklore of this unique region.

Windermere, 1975

=◦1◦=

The
Supernatural

IN HEATHEN times, giants and giantesses figured largely in the beliefs of both Celtic and Norse peoples, who after their conversion to Christianity recorded many of the old ideas in stories, poems and sagas. These myths, being but imperfectly remembered at the time they were written down, do not give an accurate or full account of pagan superstitions and folklore. Nevertheless, changed and perhaps garbled as they were, the ancient belief in giants, trolls and elves, in fairies and fiends, and in the Devil himself as living entities, remained a potent force for centuries. They are still mirrored today in place names for, wherever the true purpose of ancient earthworks, of grave mounds, or Roman forts had been forgotten, the local folk around ascribed their construction to superhuman beings, so that the folklore of most counties has provided the names for many ancient sites. Consequently, historians and archaeologists know that where popular imagination has named places after the devil, or other supernatural beings, or after some cult hero like King Arthur, Puck or Robin Hood, remains of considerable interest may be looked for there.

Sometimes, of course, tradition has ascribed outstanding natural features to the devil, or to giants or witches. An awe-inspiring gorge or chasm, rocks dizzily balanced or weather-worn into strange shapes have received a supernatural name, but usually such a nomenclature betokens remains of man-made monuments. More obscure names like Thrushgill, north of Kendal (from Old Norse, *purs*, giant), Gramskew, near Kirby Stephen, (O.N. *gram*, devil and *skeugh*, wood), Tow Top, near Bampton, (*taufr*, witchcraft) and Trough Gill in Cliburn, (O.N. *troll*), remain as witness to folklore once associated with these places but in some cases now forgotten.

In Cumbria many giants' graves remain. At Standing Stones Farm near Kirksanton is a large tumulus where — legend explains — is the grave of a giant killed in battle. The Giant's Chair, a natural rock formation, can be seen in the near-by cliff. Two upright stones, sole survivors of a former complete circle round the tumulus, point to a prehistoric interment there. Rectangular moated hillocks north of the park enclosed by Lord Wharton in 1559 near Ravenstonedale are also called Giant's Graves. The latest theory about these is that they were artificially constructed rabbit warrens to facilitate the introduction of the rodent into a rabbitless district. To the folklorist, the most interesting giant's grave in Cumbria is that marked by a group of four hog-back tombstones set between two mutilated cross shafts in Penrith churchyard. Near it is the Giant's Thumb, a tenth-century cross with a broken wheel head. This giant was the traditional Sir Hugh Cesario who was associated with the caves of Isis Parlis on the north bank of the Eamont, near Honeypot Farm, Edenhall. Sandford, writing about 1670, states that a stranger came to Penrith and stayed at the Crown Inn. He was actually the historian, Camden, who visited the Crown in 1599. On asking his host to bring a 'discreet master of the town to sup with him', Mr Page, the local schoolmaster was produced, whereupon the stranger

drew forth a paper that said Sir Hugh Cesario lived at a desert place in a Rocke; a marchall man; like knight errant; killing monster, man and beast. The place he lived in caled Isey perlis, wher a little from thence is 3 vaultes in a rocke, 100 men may live in; and he was buried in the north side of the Curch ith green feild . . .

Mr Page took the visitor to the church and Sandford continues:

> on the North side ther is 2 crosses distant the Lenth of a man, one at head, and other at feet. And was opened when I was a scoller ther: by William Turner & there found the great Long Shank bones and other bones of a man, and a broad Sword besides fonde then by the Church wardens.

We are not told whether this stranger visited the caves where in 1914 the Rev. A. J. Heelis reported:

> A carved figure on the rock, perfect to this day, with the exception that the head has disappeared. (It) was supposed to record the tradition of a maiden, who, straying too near the caves, was surprised by the giant, but escaped by a long leap across a chasm.

I visited the caves in March, 1973, descending the steep bank by a series of steps cut in the rock, and examined the two caves to the right. They are situated at a height of some 20 feet above the river. The path beyond has partially fallen into the stream. The third cave is some 100 yards in the opposite direction and perhaps six feet above the river. Neither in nor near the caves could I find any 'carved figure'. The red sandstone weathers easily, so perhaps in the intervening 60 years from 1914 it has been worn away.

There are three versions of this giant's name, one gives it as Sir Ewen or Sir Hugh Cesario, another, 'One Isis, a giant', while a third calls him 'Tarquin, a giant', which is probably a late variant of the Norse name Thorfinn. W. G. Collingwood has suggested a partial solution of this problem. An authority on early northern crosses, he dates the wheel-headed cross in Penrith churchyard known as the Giant's Thumb to the period when Eugenius or Owain was king (c. 920-37) of the revived British Kingdom of Strathclyde, of which north Cumbria was a part. Now Owain's name was in old Cumbrian, *Eugein*; to the Scots, Eog(h)an, pronounced when Anglicized, like Hughan; in Cymric it became Ewain, or Owain. There was, however, an earlier Owain who, with his father, Urien of Rheged — the kingdom corresponding roughly to modern Cumbria — became during the sixth and early seventh centuries, heroes of the British resistance to the Picts, Scots and Angles. These two, with other native rulers in the north and west were regarded as carrying on the Caesarian power during the centuries after the Romans had left Britain. Hence, the legendary giant of Penrith — Sir Hugh or Owen Caesarius — is the outcome of a mingling in popular folk memory over the centuries of two heroic British champions, Owain Caesarius, son of Urien of the fifth and sixth centuries and that of Eugenius or Owain of Cumbria and Strathclyde, during the revival of British combined with Irish Norse resistance to the English in the tenth century. The confusion in popular memory of the seventh century Owain, son of Urien, with the tenth century Owain is demonstrated in *The Dream of Rhonabwy* in the *Mabinogion*. *The Dream* was probably written in the twelfth century and tells of the battle of Caer Badon (traditional date 516) when in the dream the hosts of King Arthur were allied with the Ravens of Owain ab Urien. The Ravens were obviously the Norse who aided the latest Owain against Athelstan at Brunaburh (937). By the time *The Dream* was written the two Owains had become merged in folk memory and around Penrith both were remembered as the mythical hero Sir Hugh Caesarius.

J. Walker, in 1858, pointed out that the place name *Kemp* is often applied to graves and howes in Cumbria. The word from the Anglo-Saxon *cempa* means a warrior or champion. The brow and road leading from Penrith towards King Arthur's Round Table is known as Kemp-ley. Bishop Nicolson also records 'One little close nigh the churchyard (in Penrith) is called Kemp-garth'. Then, within the churchyard itself are the 'Giant's Grave and Thumb' and Owain or Hugh Caesarius was known to Camden as 'a marchall man, like a knight errant'. In 1671 Sir Daniel Fleming calls him Sir Owen Caesarius and Sandford about 1675 refers to Sir Hugh Caesario. Collingwood suggested that the figure on the east face of the Thumb may represent the 10th. century Owain's father. The later Owain's cousin, daughter of Constantine, King of Scots, married the Viking Olaf Guthfrithson, King of Dublin, who, though a historic character like Owain, also became a legendary hero. Olaf, with his allies, Owain and Constantine, supported by a large fleet and host of his Dublin Vikings, met Athelstan, the English king at Brunanburh, thought by some scholars to be Burnswark, on the north eastern side of the Solway, where Athelstan won a resounding victory. Owain is reputed to have become a hermit after the battle. Now the caves of Isis Parlis or the Giant's Caves near Edenhall are traditionally regarded as the abode of hermits from the time of St Ninian (fl.397) and later. So that it is quite feasible that Owain or the Giant Hugh Caesario ended his life there. He is also associated with Arthurian romance, not only as in the *Dream of Rhonabwy*, but in other northern poems as the giant lord of Castle Ewain, north west of Penrith. These stories will be related in a later chapter.

Owain's son Duvenald – corrupted to Dunmail – succeeded as King of Strathclyde and continued the British resistance to the English by supporting the Norsemen. This caused Edmund, who had succeeded his brother Athelstan in 939, to invade the north-west and the chronicler states that 'Edmund ravaged all Cumbraland' and gave it to Malcolm, King of Scots. Edmund's order for the blinding of Dunmail's two sons indicates the English king's fury at this resurgence of British nationalism under the 'giant' Owain's son. The cairn on Dunmail Raise, north of Grasmere, is traditionally regarded as the symbol of this effort of the Cumbri against their ancient foes, for Dunmail was not buried under the cairn at this time, as is often stated, but ruled Strathclyde again for many years, dying at last in Rome when on pilgrimage. There is a tradition that the king's crown lies beneath the waters of Grisedale Tarn in the shadow of Helvelyn. Symbolic gestures were commonly used in medieval times, so perhaps Dunmail ceremonially cast away this insignia of royalty before exchanging it for a pilgrim's staff. Machell in 1692 visited the cairn and drew it as a huge heap of stones with a wall over the top to mark the boundary between 'Cumbraland' and Westmorland. He stated it was seventy two yards in circumference. By 1860 M.E.C. Walcot reported the cairn was so small and unshaped as to need to be pointed out. Today, after the construction of new roads, the cairn stands out clearly on the bank between the double carriageways on the summit. But Dunmail's name given to the Raise by our distant forbears testifies to their remembrance of Hugh Cesario the Giant and his son, as heroes of British and Norse resistance to the English.

The exploits of the Troutbeck giant – Hugh Heard – who lived at a much later period have been recorded by two local antiquaries with an interval of a century between them. The first, the Reverend Thomas Machell, visited Troutbeck in 1692 and tells us that 'the curate gave me a good account of all things'. Two days previous to this visit, Machell had been the guest of Sir Christopher Philipson who lived on Longholm, now Belle Isle, in Windermere. Sir Christopher also owned Troutbeck Park where 'the little estate Lowick How, lately belonged to the yeoman family of the Heards' (sic) who paid rent to Sir Christopher. Machell informs us that the Knight had supplied him with information about Windermere. He may therefore have helped him with regard to the 'giant whose family held their land from the Philipsons'.

Our second authority is James Clarke, a surveyor of Penrith, who gathered his information around 1786 from the church register and from the memoirs of William Birkett of Kentmere who appears to have been born — according to a letter of Miles Birkett — around 1682. It is interesting to compare the two accounts, as that of Clarke demonstrates not only the lapse of folk memory, but also its tenacity, together with an accompanying tendency to express details of an old story in up-to-date idiom, rather as Renaissance artists portrayed Greek and Roman characters in the contemporary costume of their own period.

We give Machell's account almost verbatim. He writes:

The report goes that, before the union with Scotland, one Heard, a man of prodigious strength and stature, upon an incursion of the Scots . . . took his bow and quivers and went alone up a hill . . . to take a view of them. As they were coming down Scots rake he shot freely at them . . . and made such havoc among them that they thought it (more) convenient to retreat than encounter such archers.

(After this) 'tis reported, the King sent for him that he might see him shoot. A bow was brought to him which was none of the weakest, but he called it *spelke* (a child's toy). Then they fetched him the strongest bows they had, and Heard, taking two of their longest arrows, and at one single pull drew them quite through the bows. The King then asked him on which victuals he had been brought up. He replied with Thickgulls (which is a 'haisty' pudding made with oatmeal and milk). The King then asked him what he would have, and he only desired this little tenement called Lowick How.

Machell then describes how Heard would sit down at a marriage feast and remain at table eating with four different sittings of guests. But after these four meals he would work or travel for four days together, without eating or drinking. 'They say he went to London after one of these feasts from his own house', Machell ends — 'he died ten years ago'.

Clarke's account, embroidered in various ways, is much vaguer in others. He states that the giant's name was Gilpin, commonly called the Cork Lad of Kentmere, that he lived in the reign of Edward VI (1547-53), and that his mother was a nun of Furness Abbey, turned out for being with child. He was also told that the Lad was summoned to London, not because of his prowess in archery against the Scots, but because he had forcibly resisted the attempts of the legal owner to take possession of the cottage he and his mother were occupying.

When in London, he was admired, not for his skill in archery but as a champion wrestler. Matthew Birkett in a letter dated 1786 further informed Clarke that he had learned from a man who was 104 years old when he died that Hugh Hird (sic) for that was the Lad's name, had lifted a 30-foot-long beam, 13 in. and $12\frac{1}{2}$ in. in thickness, into place entirely by himself. Birkett also recounted Hird's exploit against the Scots.

When questioned by the King as to his diet, Hird replied, 'Thick pottage and milk that a mouse might walk upon dry shod, for breakfast, and the sunny side of a wether for his dinner.' It is doubtful from this equivocal reply whether His Majesty would understand that Hird was referring to cream and to a sheep roasted whole, since all sides of a wether are in the sun at some time. Or indeed, whether Clarke or one of his Kentmere informers was its author.

'Tradition tells us', Clarke adds, 'that Hird killed himself at the age of forty two with pulling up trees by the roots.' If however, he was born before nunneries were dissolved (around 1536) his year of birth was 1484 at the latest. By the reign of Edward VI, he would have been at least 63 years of age. Matthew Birkett carefully refrains from mentioning any king by name, a precaution which Clarke or his informer would have done well to follow. But this is one of the characteristics of folklore; dates and periods are often undependable and historic facts are given which are questionable.

Since Furness Abbey was a Benedictine house under an Abbot, how did Hird's mother come to be a nun there? There are many difficulties of this nature in both our early records. But how much we gain from them! The picture of a Border archer in action single-handed against a band of Scottish marauders, exercising a skill which won for England innumerable battles. A glimpse into the frugal life of the dalesfolk — 'poddish' and fresh milk, with meat 'when it was available'. Their lack of worldly ambition and contentment with so little. When the king asked him what he would have, he only desired this little tenement called Lowick How. It is Clarke who adds, 'The whole estate would have been granted if he had asked it'. Even Heard's apparent gluttony was in reality his forethought in preparing for the needs of the morrow's tasks and Machell expressly states that he ate with moderation and paid his groats with the rest of the company. Moreover he worked for four days without further food, having eaten four meals. His great strength was not only devoted to killing off enemies but put to the service of the community, as when he lifted the beam into place for the builders. Finally we are left with a conviction that the Cork Lad once really lived in the dale and performed there his Samson-like feats. The exact period when he lived remains unproved but also unimportant.

The place names of Cumberland suggest a singular inactivity on the part of the Devil and his minions within the county. Only the name of Fiends Fell shows that the Anglian dalesmen regarded the fierce Helm Wind that came down from the Pennine summits to have been due to the activities of demons. The Old English name Fiends Fell was in use until at least 1479. Some time later, the new name of Cross Fell points to the erection of a cross to counteract the demonic powers believed to dwell on the summit. There is a tradition that an altar was also erected up there and Bishop Gibson in the eighteenth century thought that the boulders on the top of high mountains might have been the remains of early chapels. Even today we speak of storms brewing, and certainly the violence of the Helm Wind, whirling down chimneys, uprooting trees and lifting haystacks from one field to another must in more superstitious days have suggested it was due to supernatural powers.

There is one legend, however, about the Devil's activities in the Gosforth district. Tradition says that he decided to link the Isle of

Man to Cumberland by a bridge starting from the Herdy Neb, a promontory near Seascale, but, as he was carrying the foundation stone, his apron strings broke and the boulder fell. This still bears two white stripes — the marks of his apron strings — as can be seen on Carl Crag, the name given to the stone the Devil dropped. It lies about a mile south of the Herdy Neb but has been covered by blown sand of late years.

By contrast the place names of Westmorland commemorate several of the Devil's doings. He is certainly to be congratulated on the outstanding beauty in structure and locality of his bridge at Kirkby Lonsdale, built over a rocky gorge of the Lune. Legend tells that an old woman's cow had strayed across the river. By evening, when she went to seek it, the stream was in spate. She was standing on the bank, wondering what to do, when the Devil appeared and offered to build a bridge by morning so that she could cross it and bring back her cow. The woman agreed to his price — the first living thing to cross the bridge — and went home. The Devil worked hard and by dawn his task was completed. When the woman appeared, he demanded his payment. Setting down a little lap dog which she had hidden in her shawl, she threw a bun over the bridge. The animal pursued this, and the Devil, leaving the dog unharmed, disappeared with a howl of rage; his neck collar which he had taken off in order to work more easily, he also left behind. It can still be seen down-river on the right bank between the old bridge and the new. As children, we were shown the Devil's finger-marks on a coping stone of the second recess on the right when going towards Casterton.

Writing in 1780 the Rev. John Hutton of Kendal relates that the Devil's Apron Strings, a cairn of stones on Casterton Fell, were dropped when a high wind tore the strings. The country folk said, if Satan had not dropped this load, his bridge would have been wider. A tumulus near Settle called Smeerside was known around 1790 as Apronful of Stones; these too were dropped by the Devil as he flew over to build the Bridge. A monolith — Fourstones — near Bentham, and a pile of stones at Braida Garth, at the head of Kingdale, are also reputed to have been spilled from the Devil's apron. Hollow Basin or the Devil's Punch Bowl — a huge grassy crater in a field beyond Ruskin's View at Kirkby Lonsdale — is said to be the Devil's work. For some reason, not stated, he buried an early church there so deeply that it lies below the hollow. I was told as a child to listen there with my ear to the ground and I might hear the church bells chiming. But alas! they never rang for me.

How old is this tradition regarding the Bridge? Longfellow wrote an identical story in *The Golden Legend* about the Devil's Bridge in Switzerland after his tour of Europe in 1826. The poet — of Yorkshire descent — was born in America in 1802. He may have been told the Westmorland legend when a child and later have attached the story to a Swiss bridge. Or is the Devil's name attached to all bridges over gorges which are difficult to span? Certainly the Devil's bridge in the Mynach Glen, Cardiganshire, has a rocky setting and an almost identical legend. A third Devil's bridge crosses the Hellgill Beck at Hellgill Fosse in the dale of Mallerstang near Kirkby Stephen. The legend of the Devil as a bridge builder is, however, world wide. Machell, in 1692, stayed in Kirkby Londsale and gives a full account of the town, including the bridge, which he refers to as Kirkby Bridge. Since he does not name it as the Devil's nor recount the legend, perhaps we may conclude that this was first recorded in print in 1780, with other 'devil's lore' by the Rev. John Hutton. The present bridge is considered to be of late fifteenth or early sixteenth century date. The Devil also has a Cumbrian Mustard Mill at Stenkbridge near Kirkby Stephen where an underground stream causes a rumbling sound.

The Devil frequently used witches as his agents. The story connected with the Witches Bull Pot on Casterton Fell, an awesome pot-hole, seems to have been forgotten. It is a fairly late name, which bears testimony that belief in witchcraft is a long-lived tradition. Even as late as the early years of this century Miss E. M. Ward describes how a Langdale farmer and his wife were both convinced they had been cursed. The wife felt 'as though she had a black rope round her neck'. When a gypsy called at the farm she declared she could get rid of curses. The farmer, who said the women 'had some witchery about her' agreed to pay her price — ten pounds. Later, repenting of his bargain, he had to go to law to regain his money, thereby doubtless earning another curse.

Another Cumbrian witch whose strangely worded epitaph acknowledges her unholy allegiance was Margaret Teasdale, who is buried in Over Denton churchyard. Gruesome relics, found in her house after her death proved her practice of Black Magic. A cupboard, which opened into a secret stairway, contained the skeleton of a child and the bones of a hand. Young children and the dead hand of a murderer were considered essential for certain practices in Black Magic; the hand, known as the Hand of Glory, was believed to have special powers, but only after it had been subjected to certain rites. Sir Walter Scott and Southey both introduce the Hand into their writings. Indeed, it was from accounts about this same Margaret Teasdale that Scott drew his character of Tib Mumps, mistress of Mumps Ha', in *Guy Mannering.*

Margaret's epitaph – she died in 1777, aged 98 – declares:

> What I was once, some may relate,
> What I am now is each man's fate;
> What I may be, none can explain,
> Till He that called me, calls again.

Her life was undoubtedly lawless and the Hand suggests it was used in thieving activities, for it was believed by thieves to possess the power of inducing sleep. The rites to which a murderer's dead hand was subjected are described by Douster Swivel, the German adventurer in Scott's *The Antiquary.* He declares it must be

> dried very nice in de shmoke of de juniper wood . . . and a little yew . . . ; then you do rake something of de fatch of de bear and de badger and . . . of de little sucking child as has not been christened (for dat is very essentials) and you do make a candle and put it into de Hand of Glory, at de proper hour and minute, with de proper ceremonish.

It was believed that when the candle held in the Hand was alight, those who were asleep in the house would remain as if drugged as long as the candle burned. A story from Stainmoor, just over the border from Cumbria, illustrating the use of the Hand, was collected for William Henderson in the spring of 1861 from the daughter of the servant who played a leading part in this drama.

One night in 1795 a woman traveller arrived at the old Spital Inn on Bowes Moor. Stating she must leave early and would need only a light breakfast, she elected to sit up all night by the kitchen fire. A maid was deputed to stay with the guest, however, and this girl rested on the settle. On glancing at the stranger, she saw that trousers were protruding from the so-called woman's skirt. Startled, the maid nevertheless pretended to fall asleep. Soon the traveller stood up and producing a Hand of Glory, placed a lighted candle in it, then brought the gruesome relic near to the girl's face and intoned,

> Let those who are asleep, be asleep.
> Let those who are awake, be awake.

The maid managed to retain her unconscious attitude, but when the stranger put the Hand on the table and went to the outer door, the girl silently followed. As the man stood on the steps calling for his accomplices, the maid pushed him violently into the road then shut and bolted the door. Rushing upstairs, she tried to waken the household. All remained as if drugged. Downstairs again she tore, seized a jug of blue milk and flung it over the candle burning in the Hand. Meanwhile the thieves had been pounding on the door. The noise now wakened the innkeeper, who rushed to a window and asked what they wanted.

'Give us the Hand of Glory and we'll go away', they called. The innkeeper replied with a shot from his pistol. The thieves then fled, leaving a trail of blood behind which was followed for some distance in the morning.

A more recent witch was Mary Baynes of Tebay in Westmorland. Like many old women regarded as witches she was repulsive in appearance. During the early nineteenth century, when Ned Sisson was landlord of the *Cross Keys* in the village, his dog killed Mary's cat. Ned asked Willan, his servant to dig a grave for the animal, after which Mary brought out her pet together with a book from which she asked Willan to read some verses. The man merely guffawed and tossed the cat's body into the grave calling out,

> Ashes to ashes, dust to dust,
> Here's a hole and go thou must.

Angry and distressed, Mary cried that he would be punished for his ribaldry. Soon after, when Willan was ploughing, the share caught a rock, causing the plough handle to fly up. This hit Willan's eyes and blinded him. Immediately, accusations were levelled at Mary that she had cast an evil spell on him. The days of witch hunting were past, but Mary was shunned more than ever by the villagers. Perhaps she enjoyed her notoriety. Certainly she added to it by making strange prophecies. One of these, that fiery carriages propelled without horses would one day rush up the dale above the Lune came true, for in the 1840s, within a generation of her death, engineers were building the railway beside the river, in the position which Mary had indicated. In these days when the powers of suggestion and extra-sensory perception are being investigated by scientists, who shall say that some of the powers ascribed to Mary may not have actually been authentic?

Wizards as well as witches were believed to have exercized their powers in the Lake District, among them the famous reputed magician Michael Scot who is said to have retired in old age to the great Cistercian abbey of Holm Cultram and to have been buried there about 1291. The earliest recorded tradition about Michael Scot is found in Philemon Holland's translation of Camden's *Britannia* in 1610 where David I of Scots is stated to have built *Holme Cultrain* abbey.

The Abbots thereof erected Vlstey (Wolsty Castle) ... for a treasury and place of surety to lay up their books and charters. ... wherein the secret works, they say, of Michael the Scot lie in conflict with mothes ... Michael professing here a religious life, was so wholly possessed with the study of mathematiks and other abstrus arts about ... 1290, that he was taken of the common people as a Necromancer.

Camden in his earlier edition does not mention Michael but records that Wolsty was built to safeguard books and papers.

In 1629 another writer, Satchells, visited Burgh under Bowness and stated that he was shown Michael's tomb in the church. Other traditions exist however, which make Melrose or Glenluce his place of burial. Satchells also saw 'one of Sir Michael's Histories hanging on an iron pin in the castle'. No one had dared to read it for 'Mr Michael's name does terrify each one'.

James Jackson of Holm Cultram in August 1654 recorded in his *Diary* the names of those who had just pulled down Wolsty Castle. He confirms that one room there was called Michael Scot's chamber.

About 1675 Scot was described by Edmund Sandford as 'a great conjuror' able to command the sea, by the help of demons. Mounted on a devil's horse the magician was bidden to ride towards the city but on no account to look back. Terrified, however, by the hideous noise of many waters behind him, he turned in his saddle — 'and there, the sea Stopt at Boostat hill, 8 miles from Carleile'. Hutchinson, in 1774, repeated Holland's account of 1610.

Later tradition ascribes the building of Bolton Old Church in one night to imps working for Michael Scot. The erection of rocks on Carrock Fell is attributed to the powers of either the Devil, of a giant or of Michael Scot. On both shores of the Solway the traditional account of the formation of Criffel, on the Scottish side is ascribed to the alliance between Scot and the Devil. The wizard was bound to keep the Prince of the powers of the air constantly busy so Michael assigned to him the task of building a causeway over the Solway. Satan was carrying a pannierful of rocks from Cumberland when the creel string broke as he passed over the Nith. The material thus deposited became known as Criffel in memory of the mishap the name being locally thought to have been derived from Creel Fell.

Although Michael Scot's birthplace and tomb are not exactly known, he is thought to have been born in the north-eastern Border Country. His traditional claims to fame in that region as in north-west Cumbria are chiefly due to his reputation as a wizard. Modern scholars, however, now regard him as 'the leading intellectual in Europe in the first third of the thirteenth century'. But medieval men of learning who studied at Toledo, becoming — like Michael Scot — proficient in Arabic and mathematics, paid the usual price of being regarded by the unlettered as in league with the Devil and his minions.

Belief in elves and fairies, as well as in witches, wizards and the supernatural in general, remained strong in remote districts of the Lake Counties until into the twentieth century. There are many examples of the place-name 'elf howe', which testify to the ancient belief that elves were dwellers in burial mounds, and hills. Among these are Elf Howe in Kentmere, Elfa Hills in Hutton-in-the-Forest and Elf Hall near Millom. Folk stories about late travellers who looked through a door into the brightly lit interior of a grave mound where an elfin feast was in progress are common. The Rev. H. J. Bulkeley of Lanercost Priory wrote in 1885 of a man from Bewcastle who returning home late one night was dragged off his horse and would have been thrust through a door in a fairy hill if he had not had the page of a Bible in his pocket – carried doubtless as a charm. Other charms which disarmed fairies were iron and steel, crosses and rosaries. To pass over running water or a cross-roads also rendered them powerless.

Some of the sagas appear to identify elves and land spirits with grave mounds. These beings were closely connected with the god Freyr and were worshipped in Sweden in the early 11th century. Freyr's cult was associated with fertility and the sun and also with the dead. In Cumbria, as elsewhere, from early Norse times to at least the eighteenth century, elves were feared as possessors of tiny flint arrowheads with which they killed both men and cattle. These arrowheads were believed to have been owned originally by mermaids who gave them to the older fairies for use as breast-pins; the fairies gave them to the elves, who then used them as weapons. Irish peasants adopted the fairy fashion of wearing the stones mounted as lockets or brooches to protect them from elf-shots.

The belief in elf shooting is probably Scandinavian in origin and is illustrated in the *Bandamanna Saga*. An Icelandic Viking named Hermund was at feud with a certain Egil and set out to burn his enemy's house. On the open fell the twang of a bow-string was heard and a second later Hermund felt a pain under his arm. He became so ill that his men took him home and sent for a priest. Shortly after, Hermund died, muttering 'Two hundred in the gill', apparently referring to an army of elfin bowmen he had seen or imagined.

Many accounts of elf-shot cattle occur in Scotland and Ireland and cures believed to counteract the results of the wound inflicted, vary with every district. In the north of England treatment included touching the ailing animal with another elf arrow and giving as medicine, water in which one had been washed. This explains Bishop Nicolson's reference in his diary for 27 June, 1712: 'By Cardornoc to Bowness (on Solway) where we saw several Elf

Arrows, too pretious (for the cure of Cattle Elf-shot) to be parted
with.

From a letter by the Bishop to Sir William Dugdale in 1685 we
must conclude that his 'too pretious to be parted with' was ironic,
for he then wrote: 'The natural superstition of our borderers at this
day are much better acquainted with and do more firmly believe
their old legendary tales of fairies and witches than the articles of
their creed.'

If, however, a page purporting to come from the *Register of
Deaths* in Lamplugh parish is genuine, the beliefs of some of the
Bishop's clergy in fairies, will-o-the-wisps and witches appear to
have been as strong as those of their parishioners. The old document
was found among the Lamplugh family papers and registers deaths
from *janry ye i, 1658 to Janye ye i, 1663,* and includes:

Frightened to death by fairies	3
Bewitched	4
Old women drowned upon a trial for witchcraft	3
Led into a horse pond by a will o' the wisp	1

Whether factually true or not, this document, written on ancient
paper, mirrors a period of great spiritual uncertainty and
undoubtedly expresses beliefs held by Cumbrians at that time.
In lonely farms and hamlets, far from civilisation, linked only by
packhorse or cart track with the nearest dwelling often miles away,
witchcraft and spells, elves and fairies, giants, dobbies and ghosts
were fearsome realities.

Many place names also recall fairy traditions. Near Arnside in
Westmorland are the attractive Fairy Steps and not far away near
Dallam Tower the Fairy Hole. A gorge just west of Caldbeck in the
John Peel country contains some gigantic circular swallow holes.
One called the Fairies' Kettle appears to hold boiling water when
the river is in spate. A cavern nearby, nearly 20 feet long, is called
the Fairy Kirk. Hutchinson, in 1794, recounts that 'it was the scene
of sundry superstitious notions and stories' but unfortunately not a
word of them does he repeat. Caverns, holes and deep fissures in
rocks often appear in folk tales as the entrance to fairy land. King
Herla passed to the abode of the dwarf king through a cave, and the
Ogo Hole, a cave in Shropshire was, until recently at least, known

as an entrance to fairy land. Wells too were thought to be either fairy abodes or as leading to such. St Cuthbert's Well at Edenhall is an example. The Hollow Hill and caverns are both also associated with Arthurian and fairy lore, as are some ancient ruins. The Roman remains at Ravenglass, as we shall see later, were regarded as the home of King Eveling and his fairy daughter, Modron, later to develop into the Arthurian Morgan la Fée, while Walls Castle, the ruined Bath House of the fort, was thought to be Lyons Garde, home of the fairy Lyones.

The Rev. Isaac Todd, born at Wreay in 1797, told a fairy story about Caerthannoc, an ancient earthwork above Ullswater, which country folk call Maiden Castle. The Rev. H. Maclean recorded the story in 1911. It tells that a tower was built there by a king to safeguard his daughter, as a wicked fairy had foretold her death by drowning. The girl had safely reached maidenhood but, when climbing through a window to elope with a lover, she fell into a water butt and was drowned.

A favourite haunt of fairies was near Lanercost where the country folk there claimed as late as 1885 to have heard the jingle of their faery harness as they rode down the glen on their tiny horses.

Some years earlier, in 1857, Jack Wilson of Martindale said that one moonlit night on Sandwick Rigg he saw a company of fairies, dancing. A ladder stretched up into a cloud overhead and on seeing Jack they climbed this quickly. He tried to follow but like a flash they drew up the *stee* (ladder) closed the cloud and vanished. On telling the story Jack ended 'Yance gane, ae gane, and never saw them mair'. This passed as a sort of proverb into local speech. During this century Jack Wilson's grandson endorsed the truth of the story. 'It was true, howiver; I heard my grandfather tell it many a time.'

Near Lanercost in 1900 an old man declared that tiny pipes had been found belonging to the fairies — they were evidently inveterate smokers of their own kind of weed! A large number of early tobacco pipes found on the site and surroundings of the Roman camp at Papcastle were ascribed by local tradition to the Picts. These, in turn, were regarded as a dwarfish race, 'unco wee bodies, but terrible strang' and the drinking cups or beakers, found in prehistoric graves were locally known as pixie cups until into this century.

The same informant described to Mrs Hodgson a gift of Fairy Butter which had been left for a ploughman as he was going to dinner. 'One of his horses ate it and prospered, the other which abstained, died.' In Wales, the substance found in deep limestone crevices was called Fairy Butter; in other localities that yellow jelly-like matter formed on decaying wood was also renowned as star-jelly or Fairy Butter. Our old Cumbrian informant declared, 'Tis lucky to eat Fairy Butter'; this opinion, however, is in direct contradiction of the most common beliefs about partaking of fairy food or drink. To share a meal with anyone is usually a token of friendship and in the case of fairies, or in relation to the supernatural world, implies being bound in some way to the host. This is a very ancient idea. Because the Greek Proserpine had eaten half a pomegranate in the Underworld, she had to live there for six months of the year.

Pluto's realm like fairy and elf-land is associated in myth with the abode where the dead dwell. Among the pagan Norse it was believed that the dead lived on in the howe guarding their treasure, indeed fighting with any thief who attempted to steal it. The *draugr* or spirit of the dead man was regarded as having the same traits as the living character had possessed only in some cases magnified. Of a certain Hrappa, one saga relates: 'Unpleasant as he was to deal with when he lived, the more so did he become when he was dead.'

Many *draugr* came back to kill both men and beasts and to destroy farm buildings by 'riding' on them. The only sure way to destroy a ghost was to burn its remains. Whether our Norse ancestors in Cumbria held the same beliefs as those depicted in the sagas or not it is certain that after conversion to Christianity, they did not entirely discard their former gods, ideas and customs as the Gosforth cross, discussed later, with its portrayal of Norse and Christian story, shows.

Some of the Lakeland ghost stories probably reflect in distorted fashion memories of the Norse *draugr*. That of the Skulls of Calgarth has vengeance as its theme. Clarke, about 1788, states that:

two human skulls ... were said to belong to persons whom Robin (Philipson) had murdered and that they could not be removed from the place where they then were; that when they were removed they always returned even though they had been thrown into the Lake, with many other ridiculous falsehoods of the same stamp: some person has lately carried one of them to London and as it has not found its way back again, I shall say no more on so trivial a subject.

In 1819 William Green in his *Tourist's New Guide* stated that there was only one skull and that had nearly mouldered away. This confirms Clarke regarding the number of skulls remaining. In 1858 Alex, Craig Gibson, poet and writer, retold in dialect verse the story of the Skulls heard from John Long, ferryman for Ben Bills, Landlord of the former Ferry Inn, now Ferry House on Windermere. He related how Myles Philipson of Calgarth Hall coveted 'a lile bit farm of Kraster and Dorothy Cook' who refused to sell it to him. Philipson invited them to a Christmas party and later accused them of stealing a silver cup, which Philipson had planted in Cook's house. It was later found there. Kraster and Dorothy were, in consequence, hanged, but when sentenced, Dorothy cursed the Philipsons and Calgarth:

> An' while Co'garth's strang wa's sall stand,
> We'll ha'nt it neet an' day,
> Ye s' never mair git shot on us,
> Whativer way ye tak'.
> Whativer plan or geeat ye' try
> Ut banish us away,
> Ye'll hardly kna' we ivv away
> Afooer ye see us back.

Ever after the skulls returned to a wall niche on the staircase at Calgarth Hall, no matter what was done to destroy them. John Long claimed that 'scooers o' foak ha' seen 'em theear' before Bishop Watson (d. 1816) who bought the Calgarth Estate, had them walled up in their niche. The curse certainly came true – the Philipsons never prospered after it. Gibson testifies in a note to his poem that he heard several old people declare they, too, had seen the skulls.

J. P. White (1873) states that a burial ground was 'anciently attached to Old Calgarth and human bones have frequently been turned up there', which may have given rise to the story of the irremoveable skulls. W. G. Collingwood adds that the ancient name 'le Calvegartrige' (1390-4) from its resemblance to Calvary – the place of the skulls – may have started the legend. Perhaps the fact that the Philipsons were ardent royalists in the seventeenth century gave rise to a 'Roundhead' propaganda story against them. Certainly their support of the Stuarts contributed largely to their loss of estates and wealth.

The Legend of the Crier of Claife concerns the old row boat ferry which plied between the Nab and the Ferry Inn where the modern ferry now crosses Windermere. One stormy winter night, the Ferryman crossed in response to wild cries from the Nab. When he returned, horror struck and speechless, he collapsed and died without telling what he had seen. The restless spirit which continued to call on wild nights, was at last exorcized and laid in Claife quarry, about which many eerie tales are told.

Alexander Craig Gibson claims he heard the wind rush across the southern half of Windermere from Gummershow one wild night with a sound startlingly suggestive of the cries of human beings calling for help. He suggests that this may have given rise to local stories of the Wild Hunt or the Gabriel Hounds a tradition which Wordsworth makes use of in *The Prelude*. The long drawn out howl of a dog is in Cumbria still regarded as presaging death, and to see a boggle in the form of a black dog was in Westmorland at least, a sure sign of disaster. Henderson relates the story of one of these 'black dog' boggles which frequented roads and lanes round Beetham. It was believed to inhabit the barn at Cappleside Hall (misnamed by Henderson 'Capplethwaite') near Beetham. It took the form of a huge black dog with blazing eyes and was known locally as a Cappel. Although, like other Cappels known in Yorkshire, it was friendly to the farmer who sheltered it and aided him in his work, it was malevolent to his neighbours. Once, when the Beetham Cappel was helping to gather sheep, it chased a hare into the barn and exclaimed, 'That sheep runs very fast'. Finally the vicar of Beetham exorcized the boggle and drove it into the Bela river.

The name Cappleside is derived from *Kappall* – horse – and *heafod* – hill. Scholars think that the legendary Cappel originated in Welsh and early British folklore and is of pre-Norman origin. Jean d'Outremeuse of Liège, writing before 1400, tells in *Ly Myreur des Histors* how Ogier the Dane in 896 was shipwrecked some nine days sail from Cyprus and there fought a *capalus* – the Welsh *Cath Palug* – and other monsters. Arthur and Gavain then attacked him, but Ogier was rescued by angels. He was welcomed by Morghe (Morgain) to her palace and lived there happily with her, Arthur and Gavain. The story of Palug's Cat is also told in the Welsh triads of pre-Norman date and is believed to have entered French romance as a *Chapalu*.

The Barn, originally believed to have been the home of the Beetham Cappell was all that remained of the medieval Hall of the Middletons after 1763.

After 1687 Cappleside Hall was demolished except for the tower. In 1715 George Hilton who had joined the Jacobites hid in the ruined tower when he was a hunted fugitive after Preston. Perhaps the legend of the tower being haunted started then. The building became a barn in 1763 and another legend of a 'Cappleside leddy' haunting the tower is told in the *Beetham Repository*. All that is left of the tower now is a single wall.

From his helpful character, the Cappel has affinities with the *hob* who is also recorded in the Lake Counties. Millom Castle had a hob about whom many tales were told. He was described as having a body 'aw oiver rough'. His favourite bed when the servants retired was on the hearth, but he loved to perform tasks overnight for his family. A servant who put butter in the churn and said, 'I wish Hob would churn this', would find the butter ready set in the morning. The Hob resented criticism, however, and repaid it with some malicious trick. One farmer fearing rain next day, said, 'I wish t' corn was safe in t'barn'. He found his wish fulfilled in the morning, but a stag, Hob's helper, had found the pace too hard and lay dead at the barn door. When the day turned out sunny, the farmer said, 'Drat that Hob! I wish he was in t'millpond'. But he found his corn in the millpond the following morning! Gifts to a hob, especially of clothing, were taboo. If made, he left the farm for ever.

Mention should be made of Dobbie Stones which are reputed to have power against supernatural agents and forces and are also able to return home if taken away. One of these can still be seen at the fine old seventeenth century Bleaze Hall, now a farm in Old Hutton near Kendal. The Dobbie is a prehistoric stone hammerhead with three faces and a central socket hole. It hangs in the attic and presumably keeps in subjection the spirits of the ghostly funeral procession of a daughter of the medieval house who died from sorrow when her lover failed to return from the Crusades. The cortége has been seen to pass round the Hall but not by Mr Robinson, the present occupier or his family.

There are two more Dobbie Stones at Nether Levens Hall near Kendal, but unlike the Bleaze Hall example, they are both pieces of limestone with holes in the centre worn by water action. Like the Bleaze Hall stone, however, they are said to return home if taken away.

I can personally testify to my terrified belief as a child in the witch-like Jinny Greenteeth. According to the maid. Katy Wyatt, who daily took my sister and me for a walk, this monster still lived down the Back Lane at Kirkby Lonsdale. Although the slimy pool — her original home in the beck that once flowed under the lane — had dried up, Katy, a local girl, assured us that the witch still lived in Lunefield wood near by and would rush out and gobble us up if we were naughty.

Finally, mention should be made of the Penrith monster, surely unique, in that it originated with the custom of ringing the curfew. The editor of Cumbria writes: 'Penrith church bell was nicknamed "T'taggy bell". It was told to the children that if they were out after it rang, "Taggy'll get you".'

There is little doubt that belief in these supernatural powers and monsters played a not unimportant part in quelling some aspects at least of juvenile delinquency.

⟃ 2 ⟄

History in Legend
and Tradition

MANY ARTHURIAN and British place-names survive in the Lake Counties and through these both folklore and history have been preserved. Moreover, a rich vein of Celtic poetry and stories, originally composed, sung or recited in the courts of the heroic sixth-century British kings of the north and north-west – written down much later, somewhat changed and interpolated – still survives and adds to our knowledge of that dimly known period. Some of these prose tales and poems concerning the valiant struggle of these Men of the North as they were called, against Picts, Scots and English, after the end of Roman rule in Britain, are preserved in early manuscripts in Welsh libraries and elsewhere.

One of these northern poems can claim to contain the first literary allusion to Arthur of Britain – unless the line is a later interpolation. This poem is the *Gododdin* traditionally composed by Aneirin, one of a school of sixth-century bards whose better known contemporary Taliesin sang at the court of Urien of Rheged, a historic sixth-century king who ruled, it is now thought by many

37

scholars, from Carlisle. Urien and his son Owain together became the greatest Christian war leaders of northern British resistance to the pagan Angles. Their kingdom of Rheged is thought to have included southern Galloway, and perhaps to have stretched south to the Lune or even to the Ribble and east to include Catterick, for Urien was known as Prince of Catraeth – the modern Catterick.

Aneirin's poem was a lament for a band of British warriors from Gododdin, which stretched from Forth to Tees; this force was almost completely annihilated at Catraeth around 600. In the song the prowess of a British warrior is compared to that of Arthur:

> He stabbed over three hundred of the finest,
> He glutted black ravens on the ramparts of the fort,
> Although he was no Arthur.

This reference, if in fact included in the original poem, shows that Arthur was already widely known in the north. Indeed, old warriors who heard it sung could themselves have met with Arthur in their boyhood.

What may be a nearly contemporary record concerning Arthur occurs in the so-called *Welsh Annals* for AD 539 and reads: 'The strife of Camlann in which Arthur and Medraut perished.' The Roman fort of Camboglanna (Birdoswald) on Hadrian's Wall, then presumably in the north-western British kingdom of Rheged, has been suggested for the site of this battle in which Arthur traditionally fought against the traitor Medraut. No more romantic setting for this 'last dim battle of the west' could be found than this ruined stronghold, high above the wooded gorge of the Irthing. Professor Jackson says that philologically Camboglanna can be equated with Camlann. In the Celtic legend, Modron, daughter of Avallach son of Beli Mawr who was Lord of the Celtic Otherworld, carried off Arthur after Camlann to *Ynys Avallach* – the isle of Avallach – later mistakenly called Avalon. There, the British, and later the Welsh, believed that Arthur was recovering from his grievous wound. Modron, who was a water fey, became the Morgan la Fée of later legend and was famed for her healing powers.

Now it is surely significant that, in Elizabethan times, the Roman ruins of Ravenglass were locally believed to be the 'roial palace of

Eveling'. Camden, when visiting the place around 1599, reported this piece of folklore and said 'they speak there much of King Eveling'. W. G. Collingwood believed that 'Eveling must be Evelac, Avallach, as it was spoken by the Ravenglass people who told the tale to Camden, in the days of Queen Elizabeth.' Avallach is a proper name which appears in a Welsh triad where he is the father of Modron who became the legendary mother of Owain, son of Urien of Rheged. If Camlann is indeed the site of Arthur's last battle, then Ravenglass in the same kingdom of Rheged, would fit into the myth as Ynys Avallach. The wounded king could have been carried along the Military Way of the Wall to a British port on the Solway and from thence be taken by Modron and her eight sister sorceress queens by sea to their home at Ravenglass. This motif of a wounded warrior, carried by a faery to her abode to be healed, originated in Ireland, and Ravenglass on the Irish Sea, with its sheltered harbour must, from earliest times, have been in constant contact with the western island.

Another of the many names given to the Other World by the British, was *Caer Siddi* (Faery Fortress). *Caer* often denotes either a British or Roman fort or a medieval castle. Here, at Ravenglass was a Roman fort, which was not only associated in popular lore with Modron but with another water fay, the Lady of the Fountain, Lyones. John Denton, the local seventeenth-century historian tells us, claiming to quote from a 'history of Arthur, written by a monk' that Waldeive a twelfth-century north-western magnate gave to the new Augustinian priory founded by Henry I in Carlisle, 'ancient buildings called Lyons Yards ... the ruins whereof are yet to be seen, as it is thought at Ravenglass, distant from Carliell, according to that author (the monk) 50 miles, placed near the sea, and not without reason thought to be the same.' By Lyons Yards, Denton undoubtedly meant Lyons Garde, the castle of the Lady Liones, in Welsh legend, the Lady of the Fountain, whose castle was placed by Malory near to Avalon. Now Caer Siddi had its fountain and was connected with Manawyddan, and Pryderi, both inhabitants of the otherworld, described in a poem in the *Book of Taliesin* as follows: 'Well appointed is my chair in Caer Siddi, sickness and old age do not affect him who is in it; Manawyd and Pryderi know it ... around its corners are streams of ocean, and the fruitful fountain which is above it, sweeter than white wine is the drink in it.'

People of British descent were still living on the fells above Ravenglass in an early settlement there which, when the Norse arrived in the tenth century, they named the 'settlement of the British' — Bretteby, later Birkby — suggesting one explanation for the continuance of British folklore in this district as late as Camden's period. For Ravenglass, on a main route from the south, with the earliest known bridge in the district built by Edward, son of Ulf, around 1180, together with a hospital there for poor travellers, which supposes there must have been many, some of them, doubtless, travelling bards from Wales; Ravenglass, with its golden dunes, sheltering the town and harbour from storms of the western sea, also the highway to Ireland, 'commodiously surrounded by two rivers', as Camden says, furnished with the mysterious palace of Eveling which was the home of Modron and familiar to Manawyddan, with the ruins of the Bath House (still standing today) and in the days of Elizabeth regarded as Lyons Garde, of the fairy Lady Lyones; easily reached from Camlann, a possible site of Arthur's last fight, surely Renglas (as it was called in the twelfth century) has a claim to be regarded as one of the sites of Caer Siddi, the Ynys Avallach or Avalon of Arthurian myth?

That there was in the north-west, in Norman times, a keen interest in the belief of Arthur's survival after Camlann, is illustrated by a charming story included about 1216 by one of the canons of Lanercost in their abbey chronicle. The ruins and restored church of this beautiful building are north of Carlisle, not far from Camboglanna near the 'Picts Wall' still so called at the beginning of this century — 'pict' being then and earlier synonymous in country districts with 'pixie' and 'elf '. In the Lanercost district a belief in elves lingered long and this lore was closely linked with that about Arthur who was 'tended by an elf most fair', in Avalon — Morgan la Fée, who as we have seen was originally the British Modron, daughter of Avallach, Celtic King of the Other World.

The Arthurian story told in the chronicle concerned Peter, Bishop of Rochester, who, hunting in a forest, came upon a palace and being invited within to dine, found his host was none other than Arthur. Peter asked whether the king was healed of his wounds.

'Truly', he replied, 'I await the great mercy of God'. And the other asked, 'Who Lord, will believe me when I say that today I saw and spoke with Arthur?' And he said, 'Close your right hand'. He showed it closed. 'Open it!' and from his hand there flew a butterfly. 'For your whole life,' Arthur said, 'You shall have this memorial of me, that whenever you wish for a butterfly, do as I have said, and one will appear.' This sign afterwards became notorious and men asking for a blessing also requested a butterfly, so that Peter became known as Bishop of the Butterflies.

Lanercost is linked to modern Arthurian legend through Sir Roland de Vaux of near-by Triermain; the Knight's tomb is in the ruined chancel and he figures in Scott's *Bridal of Triermain* as we shall see later.

Blencathra or Saddleback can also lay a doubtful claim to being one of the retreats where Arthur lies awaiting the summons to return and lead those expecting him to final victory against their foes. Possibly the earliest known form of the mountain's name the *Rackes of Blenkarthure* (1589) gave rise to the story.

A much earlier Arthurian tradition, in this case regarding Carlisle was recorded in 1610 by the local historian, John Denton of Cardew, who states:

Waldeive, son of Gospatrick, earl of Dunbar gave to the priory (of Carlisle) . . . a mansion near St Cuthbert's church where *at that time* stood an ancient building called Arthur's chamber taken to be part of the mansion house of King Arthur, son of Uter Pendragon, of . . . memorable note for his worthiness in the time of ancient kings.

Here are historic facts with traditional lore added, but there is evidence that Denton referred back to an authentic building called in the twelfth-century 'Arthur's chamber'; for, after Henry I had given land for a priory to be established in Carlisle, Waldeive, a north-western magnate, became one of the first lay patrons of the royal foundation and his gift of three churches in Cumberland, and a house near the church of St Cuthbert in Carlisle to the priory is officially recorded. Is there, however, any foundation for the reported existence of 'an ancient building called 'Arthur's Chamber' in Carlisle in the reign of Henry I, or is Denton merely quoting the folklore of his own day, or perhaps a tradition mentioned by the monk who wrote the history of Arthur from which he quotes whose manuscript seems to have disappeared?

Actually there is official confirmation which proves undeniably that there existed in Henry I's Carlisle a building called 'the mansion house of King Arthur' in the city. This is found in Henry II's confirmation of a charter made originally under Henry I (1099–1135) in which Ranulf son of Walter granted 'land which was around Arthur's *burh* in Carlisle, next to the house of the canons' that is the Augustinian canons, in the city. This record of the use of an authentic Arthurian name in Carlisle as early as the reign of Henry I has not been put forward before, as far as I am aware. A *burh* is the old English word for a fortified place. After the Conquest it denoted a fortified manor or mansion which every person of rank would possess. So Denton in referring to Arthur's chamber as being 'part of the mansion house of King Arthur' is using twelfth-century idiom, possibly a direct quotation from his authority – now apparently lost – 'the monk who wrote the history of Arthur' – who may have been one of the same canons of the priory of Carlisle.

This bestowal of Arthurian names on buildings whose true origin had been forgotten is found in districts where a British population had survived the Norman domination. In Devon, Cornwall and Wales, Arthur was still believed to be recovering in the Celtic Otherworld, from his wound received at Camlann; from that realm he would one day return to restore to the Britons their ancient heritage. When in 1113 monks from Laon were visiting Devon, Arthur's Chair and Oven were proudly displayed to them. Their scepticism caused a brawl, described by a later writer in 1146. Now at this same period Cumbrians were still alive who as children had been told stories of the last King Owain of Strathclyde and Cumbria, killed at Carham, in 1016 or 18, in which battle their parents had possibly fought. Moreover, the Cumbric language was spoken in the north-west until the eleventh century. Indeed the use of Cumbric numerals, used for counting sheep by Cumbrian dalesmen until the present century, could well date back to the British period, and where a native language was still used, traditional lore would have survived. It is in accord then with early twelfth-century traditions that buildings should have been named after Arthur in Cumbria as they were in other British localities.

It is most likely that Arthur's Chamber or *burh* in Carlisle was the remains of a Roman building still standing in the twelfth century. Modern archaeologists have seen there the ruins of Roman stone structures equipped with hypocausts dateable to the last quarter of the fourth century. In Carlisle, both Camden and Leland testify in Tudor times that William of Malmesbury, the twelfth-century historian, described a Roman triclinium in the city which existed in his day. The name 'Arthur's Burh' therefore proves at least that Arthurian tradition was current in the north-west at a much earlier period than can be claimed for Glastonbury where Arthur's supposed grave was not 'discovered' until 1196. Indeed, Arthur's burh was so named at least a century earlier and the existence of this Arthurian name in Carlisle is proved by documentary evidence, not, as at Glastonbury, through surmise.

This is not to claim that the tradition goes back in Carlisle to Arthurian times, but the name suggests that Arthur's stronghold and court were traditionally regarded as being in Carlisle before the romance writers placed them there, not, as often stated, that the romances gave rise to the supposition. Indeed the earliest use of Carlisle as the setting for Arthur's court by poets and writers of romance was not until the twelfth century. Marie de France, who is thought to have lived when Henry II ruled England and part of France, stated that she used old Breton traditions and stories as the foundation for her *lais*. It is in her *Lai de Lanval* that she placed Arthur's court at *Carduel* (Carlisle) as did Chrétien de Troyes in his *Yvain* (1177-81) which has resemblances to a Welsh tale *Owein* written in the same period in which the Lady of the Fountain becomes the wife of Owain. It thus appears that legends were current among the Bretons and Welsh of the twelfth century connecting Arthur with Carlisle where Arthur's burh was well known early in that century, and probably before that date and these were incorporated by the two French poets into their writings.

The bestowal of an Arthurian name on a Cumbrian building — that of *Pendragon* as given to the castle near Kirkby Stephen in Westmorland — can be traced from official contemporary documents. Before 1309 this building always appears in the records as Mallerstang Castle but in that year Robert de Clifford, Warden of the Scottish Marches under Edward I, was granted a licence to crenellate his castles of Pendragon and Brougham, and this is the first time that the Arthurian name was registered officially. The ruins of Pendragon still stand above the River Eden in the remote vale of Mallerstang, surrounded by deep ditches which the local folk of that period thought were dug to draw the waters of Eden into them. A somewhat derisory couplet, probably composed at this time mocks this attempt – made impossible by the very nature of the site:

> Let Uther Pendragon do what he can,
> Eden will run as Eden ran.

Now since Robert de Clifford renamed Mallerstang 'Pendragon', it is logical to conclude that he was the Uther of the rhyme and that he refortified and strengthened his fortress by ditches when Warden of the Scottish Marches during the period when the cult of Arthur, of courtly love and chivalry, of Round Tables, tournaments and jousts were at their height at the court of Edward I. Moreover, though the Cliffords were descended on the paternal side from Norman forbears, Robert's great aunt by marriage was the daughter of Prince Llewelyn the Great of Wales who had worn the hereditary crown, traditionally that of Arthur – the same crown which Edward I took among his spoils of war after Llewelyn had been defeated and killed. The Cliffords had in fact for several generations been Welsh border lords and had intermarried with Welsh landed families. Indeed the Westmorland Cliffords retained an estate on the Welsh border until Elizabeth's reign. Many of their servitors must have been Welsh. More than likely a Welsh minstrel was in their service in Westmorland, so that the ancient British songs, legends and myths would be brought again to the north-west – where many of them had originated – when the Welsh-Norman Cliffords and their servitors came to Cumbria. It must be remembered, also, that Plantagenet Kings had for political reasons adopted Arthur as an English hero. Robert de Clifford therefore for personal, racial and political reasons followed his king in his enthusiasm for what was originally a British cult and named himself Uther Pendragon and his castle after Arthur's father. In the recent local lore regarding Pendragon, the Reverend J. Wharton recorded in 1902 that it was traditionally believed that Uther died in the castle fighting against the Saxons who, unable to capture it, poisoned the well. Geoffrey of Monmouth may have originated this story regarding Uther's fate in his fictional account of Arthur's father. Scholars think, however, that Uther figured in Welsh poems before Geoffrey's time. Canon Simpson also recorded about 1902 that Uther was believed to haunt Shap Fell – perhaps on his way to Carlisle, for so long a British capital.

Now, Lammerside Castle, some two miles north of Pendragon is also associated in local tradition with the antagonism between Saxon and Briton and is linked with Arthurian legend. Pennant in his *Tour* of 1801 states: 'I passed a very ancient tower called Lammerside Hall, known formerly by the sad name of the Dolorous Tower. Something was told me of a Sir Tarquin and a Sir Calidos, so probably the place had been a subject of dire contention.' 'Sir Calidos' is the giant Carado of the thirteenth-century prose romance *Lancelot*. He was one of the five Saxon brothers who captured Gauvain and imprisoned him in the Dolorous Tower, because it was believed he had murdered the brother of Carados's mother. In the local form of the legend here referred to by Pennant, we again meet the Sir Tarquin who figures as the giant Sir Hugh Cesario, dweller in the caves of Isis Parlis and enquired of by the traveller (Camden) at Penrith. Here also in the Lammerside Sir Tarquin (alias Sir Hugh Cesario) is a dim legendary remembrance of the Romano-British Owain, son of Urien and of the later 10th century Owain, father of Dunmail.

Another Arthurian place name which may well date back to Robert de Clifford's time is that of Arthur's Round Table near the Clifford castle of Brougham, south of Penrith. One of the most popular institutions founded by the Plantagenets was that of the Round Table, a purely Norman invention. This was at first a social gathering of knights and included feasting and jousting. At these entertainments knights participating often assumed the names of Arthur's knights. We have suggested that Robert de Clifford had adopted that of Uther Pendragon, so it may well have been at this time that the title of Arthur's Round Table was given to the prehistoric circular earthwork south of Penrith. Certainly, in local tradition, this ancient circus was regarded as having been the scene of jousts.

Leland in 1538 tells us that 'the ruine is of sum caullid the Round Table and of sum, Arture's Castel'. In 1671, Sir Daniel Fleming stated: 'A Roman work – the country people here do think it to have been called from King Arthur's Round Table.' Stukely next mentioned it in 1725 and says, 'It is commonly called King Arthur's Round Table', and adds: 'The site is used to this day for a country rendez-vous, either for sports or for military exercises, shooting with bows, etc.' He drew a sketch of the Table showing another ring to the south, now destroyed, with men wrestling, and horse and foot races proceeding outside.

In 1773, when Hutchinson visited the site, he was induced to believe by the villagers that 'this was an ancient tilting ground where jousts had been held'. He also adds that wrestling matches had taken place in the circle within living memory. In an article written in 1882 on the earthwork, it is asked: 'How far are modern north country games descendants of those formerly practised here? Are the local wrestling, pole leaping and general strong taste for athletic sports real and important relics handed down of the condition of our forefathers?'

Sir Walter Scott, having heard or read about the joustings, made the Table a mise-en-scene in his *Bridal of Triermain*. He first utilized, however, the awful, rude Gothic appearance of the Castle Rock of St John near Keswick, with its lofty natural turrets and rugged battlements, Hutchinson records the following tradition current in 1776 about the Castle Rock: 'The natives around asserted that if he advanced (towards the apparent castle) the genii who govern the place . . . will strip it of all its beauties and by enchantment transform its magic walls.' Scott retains the magic by making the castle-like rocks the abode of the fairy Guendolen. With her Arthur stayed for three months and on leaving swore to provide fittingly for his unborn child whom Guendolen was carrying. Years later, Gyneth, their daughter, appeared to claim from the king his most illustrious knight as her husband. A trial by jousting was arranged to be held on the Round Table at Eamont Bridge. It proved a tragic occasion. Knight after knight was slain, the maid refusing to end the conflict, until Merlin, angered by the slaughter, cast Gyneth into an enchanted sleep within the castle of St John. She was not freed from the spell until Roland de Vaux dared to enter to waken her.

W. G. Collingwood, referring to a thirteenth-century document which mentions *Castelyadolfbek* as flowing at the foot of Castle

Rock, suggested that this place name points to the existence of a Norse *borg* or castle built on the Rock by a Lindolf or Liudolf. Later he discovered 800 feet up on the fell the foundations of a hall in Norse style so that the early name could incorporate the lost folk record of a castle built there. *The Place-Names of Cumberland* however state that the second element of the word is from the old English personal name *Eadwulf.* This does not invalidate the possibility of an early *borg* having once existed on Castle Rock.

It was during the fourteenth century, however, that the district from Carlisle to beyond Penrith became *par excellence* the background for Arthurian medieval romances. One of these *The Awntyres off Arthure at the Terne Wathelyne* was written about this time, Tarn Wadling, now drained, was formerly near the Church of High Hesket. As with many of the northern Arthurian romances, the hero of the *Awntyres* or adventures is Gawain. The author was obviously a native of either northern Cumbria or of the Scottish lowlands, as his authentic descriptions of these localities prove. In the story Gawain jousts against a Scottish knight who later joins the Round Table. Inglewood Forest, Tarn Wadling and the Court Thorn are all mentioned. The last, doubtless a descendant of more ancient trees, was seen by Hutchinson in 1773. He tells us that the Court of the Forest was held, by immemorial custom, at the Thorn on St Barnabas Day.

Tarn Wadling had been the centre of wonder tales at least a century earlier than the emergence of the fourteenth-century romances, for Gervase of Tilbury, who lived for some time at the court of William the Good, King of Sicily, husband of Henry II of England's daughter Joan, wrote a book of stories to amuse the Emperor Otto IV who employed him later. This was the *Otia Imperialia,* probably finished before 1211. Two of these stories show that Gervase had heard them from one who knew the Inglewood region well. The first describes a forest near Penrith, near to a public road and full of all sorts of game. In its midst, a lonely valley echoed every day at one o'clock to the sound of bells, and the natives of the region called the valley in the French tongue – *Laikibrait.* Now there is official confirmation in the Pleas of the Forest of 1285 that the tarn named *Terwathelan* was also named *Laykebrayt.* Moreover, R. C. Cox has convincingly shown that if *Laikibrait* is divided into the syllables – Lai-ki-brait, the three Old

French words so formed mean – 'the lake that cries', and the legend of a village, drowned for the uncharitable behaviour of its inhabitants, has for long been connected with Tarn Wadling. John Ritson in *The Life of King Arthur* (1825) quotes from the earlier notes of Bishop Percy who preserved the ballad *The Marriage of Sir Gawain* which concerns the wicked baron whose castle stood near Tearne-Wadling. The Bishop states: 'There is a tradition that an old castle once stood by the lake the remains of which were not long since visible. It was, however, swallowed by the lake and may still be seen under favourable circumstances at its bottom.' Hutchinson, who visited the tarn in 1773, quotes the ballad, stating its conjectural date as 'from before the days of Chaucer'. The legend – recorded in the ballad, *The Marriage of Sir Gawain* – tells how when King Arthur lived 'in merry Carleile' with 'Queen Genever, that bride soe bright of blee' he met at Christmastide near Tearne Wadling with the bold baron of Castle Hewin, who had 'a great club upon his backe'. This giant demanded that either Arthur should fight or else return on New Years day and state 'what thing it is that a woman will most desire'. Arthur was returning on the appointed day with no certain answer to the riddle when he met a hideously ugly lady 'cladd in red scarlett' who, in return for the King's promise that she should marry Gawain told Arthur that woman's chief desire was to have her own will. This proving the correct answer, Arthur was saved from fighting the giant but Gawain had to marry the ugly lady. She however, through the Knight's unfailing courtesy and the granting to her of 'all her will' was freed from a spell and her former beauty was restored.

Hutchinson also visited the site of the neighbouring Castle Hewin and described its remains in detail, adding: 'Neighbouring tenants pay to the lord of the manor a yearly rent called Castle Hewin rent. Tradition reports it to have been one of the fortresses of King Ewain, which seems to strengthen what is told of the tomb at Penrith said to belong to Ewain Caesarius.'

Local legends connected with Penrith monuments and the neighbouring caves of Isis Parlis, all associated with Owain the tenth-century king of the revived British kingdom of Strathclyde of which 'Cumbraland' was a part, have already been told. The British place name Penrith means the 'chief ford' and it has been suggested that Owain had his centre there. The curving street, Bishops Yards, and a crescent of Georgian houses, follow the line of what may have been an oval earthwork which defended Owain's citadel at the south end of which St Andrew's church now stands. Modern air photography reveals the shape of this central area adding suggestion, though not proof, that where the Giant's Thumb and Giant's Grave are situated in the church yard the Giant Sir Ewen Caesario is commemorated within the bounds of his former stronghold.

Another romance the *Avowynge of King Arthur* was based on earlier traditions. Again set in Inglewood and the Tarn Wadling district, this poem was probably sung by minstrels in halls and on village greens. Arthur and three Knights met a huge boar in the Forest and Gawain vowed to watch all night at the Tarn. Other romances have a Cumberland setting and give Gawain a leading part. Wolsty Castle, south of Silloth, and the neighbouring 'Sainte Johnes Chappel de Groyne' were once considered by certain scholars to have been the Castle and Chapel of the Green which figure in *Sir Gawayne and the Green Knight* but 'the Groyne' is now thought to have been a sea-wall which, like St John's Chapel, has disappeared.

Some ten miles south-east from Wolsty lies the site of the Roman fort of Old Carlisle — Olenacum — which is traditionally linked with a king who ruled about the time of Arthur. Gildas, a monk writing about AD 547, tells us that a British 'tyrant' invited the Saxons to Britain to aid him against the Picts and Scots. Bede, some 200 years later, gives the tyrant's name as Vortigern, while Nennius, who compiled a *History of the Britons* around 800, recounts how Vortigern, whom he calls Guorthigern, was told by his magicians to build a stronghold in Snowdonia where he would be safe from his former allies, the Saxons, who had turned against him.

Each night, however, the building materials gathered for the castle, disappeared. Three times this happened, then Vortigern's wise men decided that a child without a father should be sacrificed on the site. After long searchings, a boy born of a virgin was found who revealed to Vortigern that two dragons, one red, one white, who inhabited a pool beneath the chosen site, had stolen the building materials. The boy — Ambrosius — advised the king to build elsewhere. Vortigern, thereupon, proceeded to erect a fortress 'in the northern side of his kingdom'.

A tradition added to a later copy of Nennius' *History* stated that Vortigern's refuge was 'at Guasmoric, near Lugubalium (Carlisle) which in English is called Palmcastre'. Professor Birley adds that 'the Nennian gloss will encourage us to suspect that Old Carlisle survived for many a long year after the departure of the Romans' as a centre of sub-Roman civilisation. It is interesting, also, that the Welsh adopted the Red Dragon as their national emblem and, as the red or purple dragon had formerly figured on the Roman imperial standard, the dragon of Wales is still a symbol of former Roman rule in Britain. Indeed the British princes were for long proud to claim Romano-British descent as we have seen in the case of Ewen Caesarius. One of the earliest of these Romano-British native princes who founded dynasties and kingdoms after the Roman withdrawal was Coel the Old – Coel Hen – who ruled Rheged, now thought to have stretched from north of the Solway southwards to the Lune or Ribble, and eastwards to include Catterick. His most illustrious descendants in the sixth and seventh centuries were the historic Urien of Rheged and his son Owain, alias Hugh or Eugenius, both of whom we have met figuring prominently in the poetic myths, legends and folklore of early Britain. Both were heroes in the struggle against the English and are celebrated, as we have seen, in the poems of Taliesin, Urien's court bard, who names Llwyfenydd as one of Urien's country centres. Now the river Lyvenet which rises near Crosby Ravensworth and runs through the former kingdom of Rheged, has a ruined group of early settlements on its banks. Among the foundations of the circular huts at Cow Green and Burwens – the modern names of two of these early villages – traces of houses of a Dark Age type exist and it is thought by some scholars that here was Urien's country lodge of Llwyfenydd, midway between his main centre of Carlisle and the eastern base of Catterick, of which he is styled in early poems, the Prince.

Carlisle itself must have been founded in British times, for its early name of Luguvalium - the town of Lugutvalos - derives from that of its original founder and signified, 'Strong as the God Lugus'. The name is recorded as early as the fourth century when the Celtic god Lugus or Lug, a solar deity, was still worshipped. His great feast, that of Beltailne, was held at the summer equinox. The corresponding feast of Samhain was held at the autumn equinox.

This belief in the power of the sun and of fire persisted in the north and north-west until into modern times. Urien and Owain were, as we have seen, champions both against the pagan Saxons and against unbelievers among their own kin. Another of their battles, mentioned by Taliesin, may have been fought on the banks of the River Winster which flows into Morecambe Bay. Sir Ifor Williams thought the name derived from the Welsh *Gwensteri* (White Stream) and a whitish clay has been found in some parts of its course. Professor Jackson, however, prefers a derivation from the O. N. *vinstri*, 'left', as pointing to the position of the Winster, which runs to the left on a parallel course to the River Gilpin, three miles further east.

Another stream, Carwinley Beck, which flows into the River Esk, south of the Liddel Water in the parish of Arthuret north of Carlisle, preserves in its name that of a sixth-century British prince Gwenddolau, a kinsman of Urien. Arthuret was originally *Arfderydd* where the battle in which Gwenddolau was slain was fought in 573. A fifteenth-century account describes this as taking place 'on the plain between Lidel and Carwanolow', the modern Carwinley, probably *Caer Wenddolau,* or Gwenddolau's fort. There are two possible sites for this ancient stronghold. One is on the Liddel where the impressive earthworks, known as Liddel Strength can still be seen; the other, the Roman fort at Netherby – Castra Exploratorum – which Gwenddolau may well have adopted as his Caer.

Nothing is known of Gwenddolau from any early historical record but a Welsh poem – the *Cyfoesi* – refers to the 'death of Gwenddolau in the slaughter of Ar(f)derydd'. An early British legend, preserved in an earlier Welsh poem, the Appletrees (*Afallanau*) tells us more through the narrator of the poem, Myrddin, later to become the Merlin of Arthurian legend. He lived at Gwenddolau's court where he enjoyed 'goodly possessions and pleasing minstrels and wore a torque of gold'. For an unstated reason, Myrddin killed the son and daughter of Gwendydd, who, in another poem is described as Myrddin's sister and by Geoffrey of Monmouth as the wife of Rhydderch Hael, after Arfderydd, the ruler of Strathclyde and Cumbria from Dumbarton. Myrddin implies that Rhydderch and his supporters are his enemies and Gwenddolau's whom he describes as

Gathering booty from every border, a glorious prince,
Beneath the brown earth now he is silent.

Myrddin himself went mad during the battle and fled into the
Forest of Celidon, thought to be in the Solway region, where he
lived as a wild man of the woods 'for ten and forty years in the
wretchedness of outlawry'.

A Strathclyde legend, *Lailoken and Kentigern*, tells us more of the
battle of Arfderydd. Lailoken is identical with Myrddin. He meets
St Kentigern — then living at Rhydderch's court — in a desert place
and confesses he had caused the battle. During the fight he had seen
a host of warriors in the sky who brandished their weapons at him.
Driven mad by guilt and fear, Lailoken fled to the woods. On
meeting Kentigern he confessed his ill deeds and said that he was
soon to suffer a triple death. He therefore begged the saint to give
him the Sacrament. Kentigern complied and later the same day some
shepherds stoned and beat the wildman, flung his body into the
Tweed and transfixed it there by a stake.

We learn further from a Welsh triad, *Three Men Who Wore
Beards,* that Gwenddolau had kept two birds — perhaps sacred
eagles — which were fed on the bodies of four Cymrie daily. The
triad of the *Three Horses* also tells of certain chiefs who were carried
to see the sacred fire of Gwenddolau in Arfderryd. This suggestion
of fire worship, together with the account of birds fed on human
victims points to Gwenddolau as a leader of the pagans in
north-west Britain. Rhydderch, on the other hand, is called
'Defender of the Faith', which provides a strong religious motive for
the antagonism between Gwenddolau and Rhydderch.

Like Rhydderch, Urien's sons and grandchildren were also
traditionally regarded as leaders in the Christian Celtic church of the
period. St Kentigern himself, as we shall see later, was said to be the
son of Owain ap Urien by a princess of Lothian, while Rhun,
another of Urien's sons, was reported by Nennius to have baptized
Edwin, the Saxon king, and 12,000 of his Northumbrian subjects,
though Bede claims that it was Paulinus, Bishop of York, who
performed the rite.

One final tradition from Nennius should wind up the heroic story
of this north-western British kingdom. Up to 635 at least, Rheged
must have remained influential, for about that time the young

Oswy, king of an increasingly powerful Northumbria, married Rieinmelth, 'Queen of the Lightning', grandaughter of Rhun, son of Urien of Rheged. If this story is true it would explain why Rheged appears to have come under Anglian rule without bloodshed. Britons were obviously not exterminated or driven out of Cumbria, but remained virile enough to become part of the British kingdom of Strathclyde when another Owain became king about 930 and, ruling from Dumbarton, had a possible centre in Penrith. The monuments there, together with the place names and legends of the surrounding district still keep his memory green, as Dunmail Raise continues to record the name of his son.

During the Middle Ages many legends emerged connected with the old families of Cumbria with the object of explaining the symbols on the coats of arms of the family to which they belonged. One of the most interesting of these is the story of the Horn of Egremont. Slightly differing versions are given by the local antiquaries Denton, Sandford and Machel. The main facts, however, relate that the heir to the barony of Egremont was captured in war and held to ransom. His brother at home refused to send the money necessary to obtain the prisoner's release but instead made himself lord of the barony. Meanwhile the captive had been strung up by his hair to a beam. The chieftain's daughter, however, who loved the young man, aided by her maid, cut him down one night, but severed the skin of his scalp while doing so. The lovers fled and arrived some time later at the closed gate of Egremont Castle, where the usurping baron was feasting in the Great Hall. Suddenly, the horn at the gate which could be rung only by the rightful heir was sounded. The guilty baron sprang up in alarm, but, we are told, a reconciliation was eventually effected between the brothers sealed by the grant of the lordship of Millom to the younger.

Denton explains that the first lords of Millom bore the horn and hatterel – a scalp. The horn can be attributed to the fact that in the thirteenth century the de Lucys of Egremont were hereditary foresters in Cumberland and the bugle was the usual badge of a forester.

Among other families whose coats of arms or crests have a legendary explanation are the Musgraves with six annulets or rings on their shield; the Redmans of Levens with three cushions on their coat of arms, and the Threlkelds of Melmerby whose crest is a female bust Proper habited gules. A later interesting tradition of the Tudor period is connected with Sir Thomas Broughton of Broughton Towers, Broughton-in-Furness, who also once owned the manor of Witherslack near Grange-over-Sands. Sir Thomas fought for the imposter Lambert Simnel against Henry VII at Stoke-by-Newark in 1487 and disappeared after the battle. He is believed to have taken refuge among his faithful tenants at Witherslack until he died. The site of his burial was known in 1599 and again in 1700 on Sir Daniel Fleming's testimony. James Stockdale in his *Annales Caermoelenses* recorded that around 1825 two of his relatives visited Witherslack and had the burial place pointed out to them by the farmer's wife there, but that the undergrowth was too thick for them to examine it. Mr Michael Hodgson of Witherslack, aged 70 in 1901, stated that he had heard of a place called 'The Sepulchre' near Witherslack Hall but that he himself had not seen it. Today, the site seems to be unknown.

Another local tradition associated with a Jacobite rebellion against the Crown – the Forty-Five – concerns the mysterious 'Princess' of Finsthwaite near Newby Bridge. In 1913 a plain white cross was erected in the village churchyard to mark the grave of 'Clementina Johannes Sobieski Douglass, buried the 16th day of May, 1771', as the inscription, copied from the parish register, records. It ends: 'Behold thy king cometh.' Her names are those of members of the royal family of Poland – the Sobieskis, while Douglas was the incognito used by the Jacobite prince, Charles Edward Stuart, the Young Pretender, who made a bid to seize the English Crown in 1745.

H. S. Cowper, writing in 1899, stated that Clementina was said by the old people of Finsthwaite to have always been called 'the princess', that she arrived with two servants around 1745 and lived with the Taylors at Waterside, a house still standing on the banks of the Leven beyond Newby Bridge. Cowper adds that, 'Some of the old people of Finsthwaite laugh us to scorn if we suggest that she was not a near relative of the Bonny Prince and a veritable princess.' What facts support this traditional claim?

The names she bore were those of Johannes Sobieski III, King of Poland and of his granddaughter, Clementina Sobieski, who was the mother of Charles Edward Stuart and wife of James Edward, the Old Pretender. These facts are well known. What is not so well known is that, on her way to Rome for her marriage, Princess Clementina was made a political prisoner by the Emperor of Germany who wished to prevent the alliance. More important as bearing on the mystery of the identity of the Finsthwaite Clementina is the fact that John Walkenshawe, her father, a Scottish supporter and officer of James Edward was instrumental in freeing the princess from prison and thus enabling her marriage to the Old Pretender to take place in Rome in 1719. When in 1726 Walkenshawe's tenth daughter was born the princess stood as her godmother and the child was baptized Clementina. Marie Sophie Walkenshawe. Years later when Clementina was 22 years old she nursed Charles Edward, the Young Pretender, who had known her as a child in Rome. Clementina was staying with her uncle in Scotland, when the prince was taken ill after his victory at Falkirk during the Forty Five rebellion, which he led. There is little doubt that at this time Clementina became Charles' mistress. The tragic defeat at Culloden followed, and the prince was a fugitive. Nevertheless she announced that he had married her and it is possible that soon after she bore his baby daughter. This is conjecture, but the traditional date for the arrival of 'the princess' with two servants at Waterside is 'around 1745'.

Why was Finsthwaite chosen as a retreat for this child who bore Jacobite names? Waterside was owned by the Taylors one of whose daughters had married the leader of the Oxford Jacobites. Another daughter married James Backhouse of July Flower Tree farm. Both Taylors and Backhouses were Catholics and certain members of both families had previously been fined for attending seditious conventicles and later for refusing to take the oath to support William III. When in 1975 I called at Chapman House which is just below July Flower Tree farm to enquire about the 'princess', Mrs. Kellett showed me an eighteenth-century Madonna cupboard built into the hall, remarking, 'Catholics must have worshipped in this house at some time'. Further research might prove that Finsthwaite during the eighteenth century was predominantly Catholic and therefore sympathetic to the Jacobite cause, which would explain why the village was chosen for the retreat of a possible daughter of Charles Edward Stuart and Clementina Walkenshawe.

Another indication of Clementina Douglas' identity is the tradition that she possessed a medal which commemorated the marriage of Princess Clementina Sobieski to the Old Pretender. This may originally have been a christening gift from the Princess to her goddaughter Clementina Walkenshawe at her baptism in 1726. Now in 1754, when Charles Edward and Clementina Walkenshawe were living together in Paris, a daughter was born to them. Charles was reluctant to part with this baby and wrote: 'A *marque* to be put on the child if sent away'. Although no authentic record exists of the birth of an older daughter from this alliance, nevertheless, the medal supposedly owned by Clementina Douglas, commemorating the marriage of Clementina Sobieski to James Edward – possibly her grandparents – may have been given to her by her mother when the baby was sent to Finsthwaite to act as a *marque* indicating her lineage.

The medal is said to have been bequeathed by Clementina Douglas to her friend in Finsthwaite – Miss Penny. It is unfortunate that it has disappeared, since, taken with the names she bore and the fact that she lived and died with a family that had Jacobite sympathies, her traditional claim to be regarded as an authentic member of the royal Sobieski and Stuart lines would have been greatly strengthened.

As it is she remains a mysterious legend, one of the unsolved minor problems of history. Had Charles Edward succeeded in 1745 the 'princess' might not have remained long in Finsthwaite but, instead, have been openly recognized by 'the King from over the water' as his daughter.

— 3 —

Legends of the Saints

IT IS NOT known who first brought Christianity into Cumbria but
the earliest saint-evangelist connected by name with the region is
Ninian. Modern scholars are not in agreement about his exact dates
but the late fourth and early fifth centuries are the most likely period
for his mission work. The earliest recorded traditions about him
appear in Bede who wrote in 731:

> A missionary from Ireland, Columba, visited the northern Picts
> . . . for the southern Picts had long before as the story goes,
> received the faith of truth . . . from Nynia, a most reverent bishop
> and holy man of the nation of the Britons who had been
> regularly instructed at Rome in the faith and mystery of the truth,
> whose episcopal see, distinguished by the name and by the church
> of St. Martin, the bishop, where he himself (Nynia) and many
> other saints rest in the body, the English nation has just now
> begun to govern. The place is called in the vernacular *At the
> White House* — Candida Casa — because he there built a church of
> stone in a manner to which the Britons were not accustomed.

About the same time in the eighth century a monk of Whithorn Abbey in a poem – *The Miracles of Bishop Nynie* – described the wonders performed at the saint's tomb. Then, some 300 years later, Ailred of Rievaulx wrote his *Life of Ninian* mainly based on a lost old *Life* of the eighth century. Ailred tells us that Ninian's father was a Christian king and that on his return from Rome the saint visited Tours where St Martin, who died in 397, had his famous monastery, and that Ninian borrowed masons from Martin to build a church in Britain where he intended to work. The site chosen was 'in a place called Witerna', the modern Whithorn in Galloway, then ruled over by King Tudovallus, who, it is thought, had his centre in the Isle of Man. This ruler was at first, Ninian's enemy, but later became his convert. Some scholars suggest that Ailred may have added certain of the details he relates concerning Ninian, and the arguments regarding this view are still being put forward and continue to be contested.

It is generally agreed, however, that the traditions and place names which connect Brampton and Brougham in Cumbria with the saint go back to very early times. Both sites are, indeed, typical of the places where early Celtic Christian communities were established; both had Romano-Celtic villages within easy reach of Roman roads, near abandoned Roman forts in or near which churches, like the many Ninianic churches in Scotland, were built to serve the village population.

Brougham, in particular, was the type of place to which early missionary bishops went to strengthen and enlarge a Christian community already existing within a settled population. For there the existence of a Christian community, even before the arrival of Ninian's mission, is shown by the survival, along with altars dedicated to the pagan British god of war, of a third-century Christian tombstone. The church, situated near the Roman fort, is known as 'St Wilfrid of Brougham commonly called Ninekirks' and it is suggested that the vernacular name Ninekirks refers to the founder of the church while that of St Wilfrid denotes a subsequent re-dedication.

Some modern critics think that the name Ninekirks is later than the saint's century and doubt whether early churches were ever dedicated to saints who were not martyrs, or buried in the churches dedicated to them. But Dr Hanson points out that churches containing some relic of a saint were, during the fifth and sixth centuries, often dedicated to that saint. Moreover the name Ninekirks, in the vernacular, points to a long-standing tradition connecting the church with Ninian or with one of his early followers.

The same critics also doubt the association of St Ninian with St Martin of Tours implied by Bede: but Ninekirks, if it is indeed an early monastic settlement, has other resemblances to that established by St Martin outside Tours; for he had a cave sanctuary outside the city at Marmoutier, and the Isis Parlis caves across the Eamont from Ninekirks, traditionally associated with Ninian, are strikingly similar to those used by the Gallic saint. Here also is found, on the river bank near the caves, the Well of St Ninian, one of several in the district, like the one at Brisco in the Carlisle parish of St Cuthbert's Without, near a Roman station.

How long this British Christian community maintained its independence we cannot be sure, but the finding of a hoard of debased Roman coinage, tentatively dated to AD 600, when a grave was being dug in Ninekirks churchyard, shows that this district was still inhabited by the Romano-British at least to the end of the sixth century and indeed, as Professor Birley has said, 'If there is any site in our district where Romano-British survival may be postulated, it is here, . . . and the name suggests a survival of Roman Brocavum long into the post-Roman period.'

At Brampton the association of St Ninian with St Martin is even closer. The church there, located within the Roman fort — abandoned even earlier than that at Brougham — is dedicated to St Martin, but Salway agrees that it was most likely so dedicated in sub-Roman times. Near by is St Ninian's Well, known as Ninewells, and St Martin's Oak which could be pointed out till the end of the eighteenth century.

The British village near the fort, for whose use the church was no doubt founded, continued to be occupied for at least two centuries after the fort was abandoned; and although the Saxons, who penetrated into Cumbria in the seventh century, built a new village some two miles away from the old British site, they continued to use the old St Martin's church till a new church was built at Brampton in 1781. So that the worship of Christ seems to have been continuous on the site chosen by Ninian for at least twelve centuries.

There were two other churches in Cumbria dedicated to St

Martin. One is the chapel at Martindale which was known as St Martin's at least as early as 1266. The other at Bowness on Windermere was reconsecrated in 1483 after a fire had destroyed the earlier building. It is not known when this was built or to whom it was originally dedicated. The font, however, is probably Norman and being discoloured by fire is thought to have been used from the time when the early chapel stood here, which gives some indication of the date of that building. Machell recorded about 1692 three coats of arms in a side window and wrote 'they have a tradition that a shereman, a smith and a carryer were buried there'. Ferguson, following Clarke, referred only to the Carrier's Arms in this window. Bruce Thompson points out, however, that part of the Shearman's Arms as well as the Carryer's can still be seen and adds that presumably the Smith's Arms disappeared some time after Machell's visit.

St Patrick's birthplace is in dispute but a group of scholars believe he was born about 390, in the Solway region. This was about the time when St Ninian was traditionally believed to have been visiting St Martin in Tours. We learn from St Patrick's *Confession*: 'I had a father Calpornius, a deacon, son of Potitius, presbyter, of the village of *bannaven taburniae* where he had a *villula* nearby, and where I was made a captive. I was then almost 16.' In his *Epistle to Coroticus* Patrick adds that male and females slaves of his father's house were also captured and taken with him to Ireland. There he served as a cattle herd and tells us that his faith was deepened until, after six years of slavery, he was commanded in a dream to return to his own country and was told, 'Behold, thy ship is ready'. Patrick escaped, journeying 200 miles to where the promised ship, manned by pagans, took him aboard. Three days later they landed on a desolate coast and walked for 28 days. When near starvation Patrick prayed, and a herd of pigs appeared, which saved their lives. Eventually Patrick reached home to be warmly welcomed by his parents. At the end of this little known period, Patrick dreamt that a certain Victorinus brought a letter from Ireland. While he read this he heard the call of 'those who dwelt by the wood Foclut, which is by the Western sea, crying as with one voice, "We beg thee, holy boy, come and walk again among us".' After being consecrated a bishop, Patrick obeyed the call and never again saw his kin or his native land.

The name of Patrick's birthplace *bannavem taburniae* or alternatively *bannaventa burniae* has never been satisfactorily identified, but many scholars accept that its location was probably in Rheged or Strathclyde. Since the place name contains *venta* the distinguished Bollandist scholar Grosjean has suggested Glannaventa, the name of the Roman fort at Ravenglass 'on the western sea' as a likely site for Patrick's *villula*. Other scholars have rejected this suggestion mainly on the grounds that no remains of Roman villas have been found at Ravenglass. The site has not been excavated, but evidence has shown that there was a *vicus* or village attached to the fort, that at least one *mansio*, a building which was 'a large stone house . . . quite unlike the normal strip houses of the vicus', existed there, and if one, then excavation may reveal others. Moreover, fourth-century Roman coins have been found at the fort and a gold piece of Theodosius I (375-95), discovered at the foundation of Muncaster pele nearby, show that the site remained in occupation until the end of the fourth century at least. And since Glannaventa is the only name on the western sea-board which contains the element *venta,* it suggests this was a likely choice for Patrick's birthplace.

Another town traditionally, though not historically, connected with Patrick is Aspatria, meaning 'Patrick's ash tree', where a well once existed dedicated to St Patrick. Those seeking a cure used to hang their offerings on the tree. Another Holy Well exists at the church.

On the fringe of the Lake District, near the old village of Heysham, Lancashire, the romantic ruins of an ancient chapel, dedicated to St Patrick, with several rock-cut tombs nearby, stand on a windy headland above the sea. Like the ancient church of St Peter, below, the chapel is at least as old as the ninth century. Baines, the Lancashire historian, suggested that Irish Christians built both in the sixth or seventh centuries. But J. D. Bullock, a modern historian, regards chapel and graves as the work of Anglian monks around 810. They, too, probably built the church for the parish. After the Christianized Irish-Norse arrived in the early tenth century, the chapel was probably dedicated to St Patrick. The late legend that the saint landed at Heysham is now thought to be a myth of explanation.

St Kentigern, who died in 612 — according to tradition at an advanced age – was, like Saints Ninian and Patrick, associated with the north-west. He is the reputed founder of the Christian church of Strathclyde, centred in Glasgow, and a later bishop of Glasgow claimed that Kentigern's diocese had included the northern part of Rheged.

Most of what is known of Glasgow's patron saint is found in the *Life of St Kentigern* written around 1180 by Jocelin, a monk of Furness Abbey, for Bishop Jocelin of Glasgow. An earlier anonymous *Life*, however, dedicated to Bishop Herbert of Glasgow (1147-64), recorded that Kentigern was born of a virgin. This motif of 'the fatherless child' was not uncommon in British folklore, but Jocelin regarded it as heretical. There are other sources which refer back to earlier lore, but the story about Kentigern, as gathered from them all, describes the saint as born of Taneu, daughter of a pagan king of north Britain, after being wooed by Ewan or Eugenius, son of Urien, king of Cumbria. Ewan is described as *elegantissimus,* most graceful, and as sprung from the most ancient stock of the Britons. Professor Jackson says that Taneu, meaning 'slender', is a genuine Cumbric name. Ewen is Owain son of Urien, whom we have met before. In the earlier *Life,* the saint's mother, there called Thaney, angered her father by refusing to marry Owain and was sent to serve a swineherd who was secretly, a Christian. Owain disguised as a girl visited Thaney, who conceived by him, though he persuaded her she was still a virgin. Her father on discovering her pregnancy had her hurled from a mountain, but she was miraculously saved, only to be set adrift in a boat which came ashore at Culross, where she bore her son. Certain herds found mother and babe and reported their discovery to St Servanus in his monastery nearby. Jocelin tells us that Servanus baptized the mother calling her Taneu and the babe, Kyentyern. Servanus brought up the boy, and loved him dearly 'hence he was accustomed to call him in his native tongue *Munghu,* which means "beloved friend".' Jackson states that both Kentigern and Munghu are Brittonic names. In contemporary Latin, Kentigern is *Cunotegernos, tegernos* meaning 'lord', the stem *cun,* 'hound', an animal much admired by the Celts. Jocelin wrote that 'in his day [the twelfth century] the common people frequently call the saint *Munghu,* 'Dearest friend' and invoke him in their need'. In early British, Irish and Scottic churches it was customary to give monks pet names, and *Munghu* was Kentigern's.

Later, the saint founded his own monastery on the Clyde. He was persecuted by King Morken and his relatives of Strathclyde and fled from them to Wales, though some modern scholars doubt whether Kentigern ever visited that country. According to tradition Morken's palace was on the shores of Mockerkin Tarn near Ullock, and Jocelin states that the King was buried in his royal town of Thorp Morken. He also said that the saint stayed for a time in Carleolum (Carlisle). Here, learning 'that many among the mountains were given to idolatry' he turned aside to 'wean them from strange and erroneus beliefs'. Jocelin continues: 'He remained some time in a thickly planted place . . . where he erected a cross . . . whence it took the name in English of *Crosfeld* in which very locality a basilica, recently erected [i.e. in the 12th century] is dedicted to the name of the blessed Kentigern.' Professor Jackson thinks that this mention of *Crosfeld* and the new church by Jocelin may be due to his own personal knowledge of the ecclesiastical history in the north-west, as he was himself a monk at Furness Abbey around 1180.

Crosfeld is undoubtedly Crosthwaite, on the outskirts of Keswick, renamed by the Norse, since *thwaite* means a clearing and Jocelin referred to its thickly wooded area where the saint erected his cross. The church, though no part of the present building is earlier than the fourteenth century, is dedicated to St Kentigern. Proof that Crosthwaite has been inhabited from the earliest times was provided in 1903 by the discovery of the remains of a settlement on Bristowe Hill nearby. W. G. Collingwood states (1925) that 'these used to be regarded as prehistoric in date but now we may suspect that the remains of an ordinary British village was here'. At its northern base the hamlet of High or Low Hill possessed a well known as St Kentigerns'. This, had been filled in, but was recorded in 1903 by Canon Rawnsley as 'still remembered'.

In addition to that at Crosthwaite the following seven churches in Cumbria are all dedicated to St Kentigern, a number which far exceeds that in any other English county. Of these, Irthington, east of Carlisle, is on the line of the Wall and its military road along which Kentigern may have travelled. Here a How or Ha' Well lies within the churchyard. Grinsdale, west of Carlisle, formerly had its St Mungo's well destroyed by encroachments of the Eden. The church is also on the line of the Wall.

Caldbeck, besides having a well, was linked to St Kentigern through a magnificent folio missal given to the church in 1506 by Dominus Robert Cooke, in which the Office for St Kentigern's day (12 January), was inscribed – perhaps by the donor – on the fly-leaf. No Office for St Kentigern was included in any of the English service books, but only in the Scottish. The missal, formerly in the care of the Benedictine community at Warwick Bridge, is now treasured by Ampleforth School. On the route to Caldbeck, south of Carlisle, is Dalston with its ancient church of St Michael, near to which is a field commemorating St Kentigern by its name of Mungo croft.

Castle Sowerby church lies south-east from Caldbeck and has an ancient well, enclosed with hewn stones in the vicarage garden. In 1703 Bishop Nicolson described a north window in the church as showing 'a military person' with part of a crowned female head which, he suggests 'I take to relate to the Legend of St Mongal (sic) and Kentigern, said to be begotten on a king's daughter by an angel'. It is suggested that the 'military person' may represent the heroic Owain, Mungo's traditional father. The romance between the 'graceful' Owain and 'slender' Taneu is recalled by the existence of Thanet Well Cottage, a mile or so east of the church, mentioned in the Parish Register (XXII) of Greystoke as 'supposed to have been named after Princess Thenew.

Mungrisdale lies south-west on Kentigern's traditional route towards Crosthwaite. The church is dedicated to Kentigern, and 'the fact that there is no pre-Reformation evidence for the dedication does not disprove its antiquity.'The chalice in the church is inscribed *Mounge Grieesdell 1600* and in such a remote place traditions of St Mungo could have lingered in popular memory into Elizabethan times and, like the vernacular name given to Ninekirks, Mungo seems to have been the popular name to designate the church and district, as Mungrisdale means Mungo's dale of the pigs.

At Aspatria, there could be seen, in 1881, a doll-like bust, which, inserted into the exterior of the east chancel wall of the modern church, bore underneath the inscription, 'Sanctus Kentigernus'.

In a field to the north of the church at Bromfield is St Mungo's well, which the Rev. R. Taylor enclosed around 1890 with a circular vault of stone. Within the parish, east of Blencogo village, is a Holy Well near to St Cuthbert's Stane, while an earthwork at

Bromfield, locally known as St Mungo's Castle is medieval in date.

Wells, in early times were regarded as having their own tutelary gods and goddesses and even in Christian periods, after they had been dedicated to Christian saints, country folk still believed they were the homes of fairies. Consequently, offerings were thrown into them. In my own youth we placed bent pins on the surface of the water in wishing wells. If they floated the wish was granted. This seems to be a method used to keep away evil fairies, for when a hearthstone in Deepgill Farm near Pendragon Castle was taken up the Rev. W. Nicholls records that several earthenware jars of bent pins were found beneath it.

Until late in the nineteenth century it was a May Sunday custom to gather at certain wells and there to drink Spanish or sugar water from bottles filled with well water. These days were called Shaking Bottle or Sugar Water Sundays. In the neighbourhood of Penrith certain Sundays were always kept by neighbouring villages for the May celebrations. Skirsgill had the first Sunday in May, Clifton the second, Edenhall at the Giant's Caves had the third, and the fourth was at Dicky Bank well on the fellside at Penrith. That at Clifton was held on the first Sunday after Ascension Day and was originally the most important, since the Feast of the Ascension was celebrated by early Christians as a thanksgiving for the return of spring, symbol of the Resurrection and of Christ as the Living Water. At this season, wells were decorated with flowers, another symbol of renewed life. The custom became debased at Clifton with cockfights, wrestling and drinking bouts and was suppressed within living memory. Spanish water was drunk in Kirkby Lonsdale, and, my cousin states, in Kendal also, when I was a child, but I never heard that anyone knew why or when the custom had arisen. Possibly in earlier times a well festival had been held at St Coume's or Columba's well, the site of which was at Chapel House, now a farm, on the summit of the hill over the bridge just east of the town, off the road into Yorkshire.

The emblems on the shield of Keswick Grammar School illustrate events in the life of Kentigern. To understand these we must return to Jocelin who tells us that after the saint had been for some time in Wales a new king Rhydderch, succeeded as king of Cumbria and Strathclyde. Rhydderch was a Christian and asked Kentigern to return to the north to help him in his struggle against paganism.

King and saint met at Hodelm – the modern Hoddom in Dumfriesshire. There Kentigern preached against idols and a hill was miraculously raised for the saint's use as his rostrum and on which he planted his cross. Both hill and cross are shown on Keswick school coat of arms. There is also a fish. This illustrates the story of Rhydderch's queen, who had given a ring – her husband's gift – to her lover. The king took the ring from this man's finger while he slept and flung it into the river, then asked his wife to return his gift, which naturally, could not be found. The queen was imprisoned and in despair begged for Kentigern's help. The saint told the queen's messenger to fish in the Clyde. On obeying, he caught a salmon with the ring in its mouth and the queen was freed. Tales similar to this were told in Ireland before Jocelin's time.

The bush shown on the crest illustrates another story which is similar to certain Irish folk tales and which uses an international motif known as 'Strawberries in winter'. An Irish king having heard of Rhydderch's famed generosity – hence his sobriquet of 'Hael' – sent one of his gleemen to his court at Christmas to test the truth of the king's reputation. This jester, after playing the harp and lute at the feast, was proffered gold, silver, clothes and horses in reward. But, saying these were common in Ireland, he demanded a dish of ripe blackberries. Rhydderch at first regarded this as a joke, but rising, the man said unless his wish was granted 'he would carry off the king's honour, as the common saying is'. Rhydderch appealed to Kentigern who reminded him that during an autumn hunt he had flung his cloak on to a bush and that beneath it would now be found the required crop of blackberries. This proving true, the jester was convinced of the rightness of Rhydderch's claim to be called 'the Generous'.

The bird on the Keswick shield represents the robin decapitated by Kentigern's fellow pupils at Servanus' monastery. Kentigern miraculously restored it to life, while the bell is said to represent one which the saint brought back from Rome, though Jocelin simply states that Kentigern, among other gifts, received 'ornaments of the Church' from the Pope.

Another Cumbrian saint – Constantine – is closely linked with Kentigern, for it was through the saint's intercession that Rhydderch's queen bore a son after being barren for many years, soon after Kentigern's return to the north. When, later, Constantine succeeded as king, Jocelin states that he subdued all the barbarian nations bordering on his own people. After his death 'he was called by many, and is to this day [i.e. 1180] St Constantine'. Jackson thinks that this Constantine 'may derive from a genuine Strathclyde tradition'. The saint lived during the period when the anchoritic movement was at its height during the seventh and eighth centuries; near Wetheral, on the River Eden, three cells have been cut out of the rock about 40 feet above the water. These, described by Hutchinson, are called Constantine's Bells, and the name may well preserve the tradition of this royal hermit's retirement from the world. For during his presumed period the custom of *clericatus* was fairly common when members of ruling families, especially kings, voluntarily exchanged their secular state for that of the religious life.

By about the mid-seventh century, Rhegead seems to have passed peacefully under Anglian rule and the hermit Herbert of Derwentwater and Bishop Cuthbert of Lindisfarne are both closely connected with the north-west, during this period. The earliest written source for information about St Cuthbert is an anonymous *Life* written according to Bede by 'brethren at Lindisfarne'. This material he used for his own prose *Life of St Cuthbert,* and added to it what he had gathered 'from the unimpeachable testimony of faithful men'. Cuthbert had been granted the town of Carlisle and land around it as well as 'Cartmel and its Britons' by King Egfrith, and the saint came to Carlisle to join Queen Erminburg, who was awaiting news from the king, then campaigning against the Picts. While Cuthbert was being shown the Roman walls and a fountain in Carlisle by Waga the reeve, it was revealed to him that the king had been defeated and slain. The traditional site of the fountain is in the city market square.

Ancient paintings on the backs of the stalls of Carlisle Cathedral illustrating the life of St Cuthbert are now thought to have been copied from beautiful miniatures in a late twelfth century manuscript executed in the Durham scriptorium.

When, 200 years after his death St Cuthbert's relics were being carried by monks of Lindisfarne through the north to save them from desecration by the Danes, it was traditionally believed that wherever the cortége rested a church was later dedicated to the saint. Collingwood, however, states that 'this was a medieval fancy revived for the sake of its romance'. It would appear to be fact, however, that Bishop Eardulf of Lindisfarne and his monks, carrying Cuthbert's relics, sought refuge at Carlisle with Abbot Eadred. They also tried to cross to Ireland from Derwentmouth but were driven back by a storm and apparently landed again at Whithorn in Galloway. The romantically placed and early church at Aldingham on the shore in Furness, is dedicated to St. Cuthbert and is one of those to which his monks are traditionally thought to have carried his relics. Bede tells us that St Cuthbert was particularly venerated by St Herbert who had his hermitage on an island in Derwentwater which still bears his name. Hutchinson saw the foundations of his chapel and cell. Bede writes: 'St Herbert was in union with the man of God in the bond of spiritual love and friendship.' Each year Herbert met St Cuthbert in Carlisle but in 687 Cuthbert, having a presentiment of his own death, said that he and Herbert would never meet again. The hermit begged that his friend would pray that they might be allowed to die at the same time. The request was granted. Both died on 19 March 687, at the same hour. In 1374 Bishop Appleby ordered that the Crosthwaite vicar should celebrate a yearly mass on the island in memory of the two saints, and 40 days indulgence was granted to all who attended.

Perhaps the most interesting of the Cumbrian saints to the folklorist is the Virgin Bega of St Bees on the Cumbrian coast. Her story has all the charm and characteristics of a fairy tale and holds besides an element of mystery. It has been said that she never actually existed, but was a mythical character arising from the swearing of oaths on a sacred arm-ring, said later to belong to the Virgin Bega and kept in the Church of St Mary and St Bega at St Bees, Cumbria, and used during the thirteenth century. Canon Last has successfully argued against this theory. Moreover, legend contains interior evidence which strengthens acceptance of its underlying truth. It should also be added that the custom of swearing on a holy arm-ring was a pagan Nordic custom in vogue in the ninth century, but going back to an earlier time. That it was still used in thirteenth-century Cumberland shows the strength and longevity of pagan Norse customs in the north-west.

The earliest existing records about St Bega are contained in the late twelfth-century *Life and Miracles of St Bega the Virgin* preserved in the British Museum. The author states that his material was selected with care from the narrative of reliable men. He tells how Bega, the daughter of an Irish king, determined to remain a lifelong virgin. Her decision was strengthened by a dream in which she received from a stranger an arm-ring 'having the sign of the holy cross plainly shown on it'. Bega's father, however, determined she should marry a Norwegian prince, whereupon Bega fled across the sea and landed near the modern St Bees 'in a wooded region'. Here she settled as a hermit, performing good works until, frightened by pirates, she again fled.

Now Norse colonies had settled in Ireland by the ninth century, so that Bega's proposed marriage to a Norwegian prince would fit a date around 850. There probably existed on the Copeland coast where she landed, a primitive Christian community; for the name Preston, 'priest town', was given by Anglians to land between the modern St Bees and Whitehaven, and this was granted to the Priory of St Mary and the Virgin Bega at its foundation in 1120; the deed mentions Bega by name, so that she was regarded as a historic person before this date. Her arm-band, however, was not officially recorded until the early thirteenth century when in six charters it is specifically referred to as 'the bracelet of the blessed Virgin Bega, kept in the priory church' on which oaths were taken. Now L. A. S. Butler has convincingly argued that ancient silver arm-bands of a flat ribbon type bearing a St Andrew's cross 'plainly shown' were current in the late ninth century and have been found in Ireland, England and Scotland, which gives authenticity to St Bega's bracelet. As no deeds exist recording the swearing of oaths on the bracelet after 1300, Butler suggests that the relic may have been stolen during the Scottish raid under James Douglas when church vestments were taken from St Bees.

The early *Life* does not mention that Bega was shipwrecked on the Cumberland coast, or that vows were made or a nunnery founded. These details were added later and recorded by Edmund Sandford about 1675. He also embroidered the account given in the *Life* about a dispute between the local Meschines family and the Priory, concerning land boundaries. The *Life* tells that St Bega indicated the true extent of the lord's land by covering it with snow while the Priory lands received none. Sandford, referring to 'the Cronicles (sic) writes: 'There was a pious religious Lady Abbess and some of her sisters driven in by storm at Whitehaven and ship cast away i'the harbour.' The Abbess begged help from the Lady of Egremont whose lord promised to give the nuns as much land as snow fell upon the next morning 'bein midsumerday'. On rising he looked out and saw the land for three miles to the sea was covered with snow. 'And thereupon builded this St Bees Abbie and gave the land was snowen unto it and the town and haven of Whitehaven' with other dues and further lands.

The *Life* refers to an annual celebration on the Sabbath of the Eve of Pentecost in honour of tokens of the sanctity of the Holy Virgin found there. Tomlinson, who translated the *Life* in 1842, stated that communicants came at that date to St Bees from miles around at Easter to celebrate Holy Communion and give offerings. There was a St Bega's well, now covered in, near a field known as Chapel Howe, on the low road to Whitehaven on the summit of the hill about a mile from St Bees.

⤚ 4 ⤙

Symbols, myth and folklore
from Pagan and
Christian monuments

IT IS WELL known that symbols found in temples and churches, on funerary monuments and on cult objects throughout the world are the visible and outward signs of some of the most deeply rooted beliefs and traditions of the people who made them. On some of the stones of the prehistoric circles and barrows in Cumbria certain symbols have been incised. These are mainly single or concentric rings, some with a spine running through the middle, some with a cup at their centre, with other cups – probably used for libations – cut on the stone, while many are simple spirals.

One of such stones showing these symbols can be seen in the Maughanby circle known as Little Meg. On it a spiral runs off the outer rim of a circle with five inner concentric rings. A rough 'trinity' symbol is cut into a stone of the Glassonby circle, one complete concentric figure with two incomplete concentric circles running off it. This figure bears some resemblance to the three beautifully cut adjoining spirals (not rings) on the threshold stone of the New Grange tumulus in Ireland. There are many rude spirals on a stone of the tumulus at Old Parks, Kirkoswald. One of the Long Meg stones displays a number of concentric rings with snake-like lines attached.

The spiral symbol is allied to that of the maze or labyrinth and, as we shall see, labyrinths used to be cut in the turf on the Cumbrian shore of the Solway. All these signs have been used, together with the circle, from the earliest times to represent and also it was believed to ensure, immortality. They are found, not only on prehistoric monuments in Europe, Mexico, China, India and Egypt, but on coins and works of art, and in the manuscripts of early civilisations, as well as on later monuments and pottery, in books and paintings. The most famous labyrinth is thought to have been built in Crete with passages leading to a central chamber where the Minotaur, with the head of a bull and a man's body was finally slain by Theseus, Prince of Athens. Considerable light is thrown on the beliefs and traditions of primitive people concerning spirals by those which were tatooed on the faces and bodies of Maories right up to modern times. They traditionally believed that the soul after death met with an ancient hag who, after devouring the spirals, gave the soul the 'vision of the spirits'. Without the spirals, the eyeballs would have been devoured, rendering the soul sightless and so unable to see the spirits or to gain immortality.

W. F. J. Knight has convincingly argued that the circle, the spiral and the maze were used as magical means for protecting what was enclosed – whether body, building or city – from evil influences. The circle, especially when in concentric rings, as on many prehistoric stones, was a symbol of power and protection, as the sign of the cross is to the Christian. Sometimes two concentric circles were made in the structure of burial mounds as in the majority of those in the West. There may also have been an encircling of the tomb in burial rituals after the body had been placed in its circles of stones. The circles and spirals on the stones themselves were thought to be additional safeguards for excluding evil, as well as inducements to keep the spirit within its tomb, for it was considered important in earlier times to ensure that ghosts of the dead did not trouble the living. Professor Thom, who has been surveying and investigating the megalithic monuments of Britain for over 30 years, is also convinced that cup, ring and other markings of prehistoric origin hold a definite meaning. He has shown that in many cases, so called circles are elliptical or egg-shaped; he has calculated that a megalithic yard and inch was used in their construction, as well as Pythagorean type triangles for placing the stones. He also suggests that the circles and stones were used for making lunar observations and recordings with especial emphasis on forecasting the occurrence of lunar eclipses.

Now maze patterns also are found on prehistoric stones. These were portrayals of the labyrinth which is merely a complication of the simple spiral and could symbolize the cosmos, the world, the individual life, the temple, the town, the man, the womb, the Mother (earth), the convolutions of the brain, the consciousness, the heart, the pilgrimage, the Way. Knight has also shown connections between the labyrinth and maze and the Trojan Game which was a ritual performed by armed horsemen in early Italy. Maze rituals are known to have been connected with solar ceremonies and many mazes have been called Troys. In fact, certain towns in Europe took the name of Troy from the fact that they were built near mazes. Labyrinths were also portrayed in mosaic or on tiles in some medieval churches and are thought to symbolize the narrow and difficult Way through life for the natural man journeying towards his spiritual centre, Christ or the Holy City. These mazes are also thought to have been used for penitential purposes.

Now the name for a maze in Wales is *Caer Droia* and it has been suggested that the word *droia* is connected with *troi,* the Welsh name for the ancient city in Asia Minor. It is interesting to find that several labyrinths known as the *Walls of Troy* were cut by local herdsmen in the turf on the Solway, Cumbria. Two in Rockcliffe parish were reported as having been made or, more likely, re-cut by Christopher Graham, son of the herd of the marsh, about 1815; the other was made by Robert Edgar at a later date. The latter was still in existence in 1884, though partially overgrown. It was seen and recorded by R. S. Ferguson, who found on enquiry locally that no one knew for what purpose the turf mazes had been cut. Graham's maze was near the cottage of Will Irving, who was known as Will of the Boats, from his acting as guide and ferryman for those using the ford across the Esk, which lay on the old main road from Carlisle to Glasgow, before the metal bridge was built further east. Ferguson suggested that these Cumbrian mazes were introduced by foreign sailors who came on boats up to Rockcliffe and Sandfield, ports which then catered for craft of up to 80 tons burden. But the fact that the mazes were cut by local herdsmen points to a custom of long standing. It was well known to Captain Mounsey of Rockcliffe in his boyhood, which, according to Ferguson, carries these mazes back beyond the days of Graham and Edgar. Indeed many mazes were in use for recreational purposes in several counties of England in the eighteenth century, and as they were still being cut at Rockcliffe by local men in the early nineteenth century the custom is linked, with other similar English customs, to the earlier period. Mazes in England were also called 'Mizmaze', 'Julian's Bower' and 'Shepherds' Race', as well as 'Walls of Troy' and 'Troy Town'. May Eve games, the treading of the maze, fairs and feasts are recorded as taking place near English mazes. Those at Rockcliffe, being near a dangerous ford on a main road, may have been used in some of these ways by travellers while waiting for Will of the Boats to take them across the Esk or for the tide to go down. Moreover Will's house was also an inn and supplied drink, as a doggerel rhyme outside the cottage proclaimed after Will's day:

Now though Will's works is done an' Will himself lies quiet,
Yet lives his Spirit here. Step in an' try it,
Nor Brig nor Rail can half so pure supply it.

Perhaps the maze was the equivalent of the dart board in modern inns for those travelling on the Carlisle-Glasgow road. We know from Shakespeare's plays that mazes were used for recreation. Pliny indeed refers to them far back in Roman Italy as 'formed for the entertainment of children' and it has been suggested that the Romans introduced them to Britain. The name of 'Julian's Bower' for a maze strengthens this supposition. It is derived from the name of Julus, son of Aeneas, whose games are described in the Aeneid as being performed on horseback in a series of sinuous windings. Only one Julian Bower is recorded in Cumbria, in the parish of Brougham. Nicolson and Burn associate it with Julian of the Bower, mistress of Roger de Clifford for whom he 'built a little bower hard by Whinfell which still bears her name'. But this name is elsewhere associated with ancient earthworks, especially if these were in the form of a labyrinth or maze. Now Whinfell Forest, near Penrith is not far from Mayburgh and Arthur's Round Table – both ancient earthworks – and the latter is associated with maidenhood. Mayburgh means 'maidens' fortification and the word 'maiden' occurs in references elsewhere to prehistoric earthworks. It is suggested in *Westmorland Place Names* that, like Julian's Bower, such sites were associated with games in which perhaps maidens took part. Nicolson and Burn, about 1777, state that 'the Whinfell *Julian's Bower* still bears her name', and in 1807 Hodgson in his *Description of Westmorland* recorded that only the foundations remained of what had been in Lady Anne Clifford's time 'a spacious and interesting building' to which she sent her guests to lodge on occasions. The outbuildings were turned into a farm house, still known as Julian's Bower, after the main building had been demolished.

It is appropriate here to recall the children's game of hopscotch, played by the writer in Kirkby Lonsdale around 1910. For this, a spiral was drawn on a paved area. The rings were divided into sections and the central chamber was called 'Home'. A flat stone has to be pushed from the entrance to the home by hopping on one foot. If the stone or foot rested on a division between the sections or if the raised foot touched the ground the competitor was 'out'. In Germany the game is called *Tempel* or *Himmelhupfen,* 'temple or heaven hopping', in France it is known as 'marelles' or *'le colimaçon'* the snail. On an old drawing of a French spiral the centre is marked 'Paradise', while one section is marked 'Hell' and another 'Temporary Altar'. Possibly the stone had to by-pass Hell, while before the Temporary Altar the competitor may have been allowed to stand on both feet and rest. Children's games appear to have a common origin and they often preserve religious ideas and myths which have long since vanished from practice or remembrance within the society to which they belong.

The ancient place names given to many of the Cumbrian circles and cairns also demonstrate ancient attitudes. When an old religion was discarded, converts often retained their veneration and awe for temples, sacred stones, trees and wells dedicated to the old gods. Priests of the new religion found it politic, therefore, to 'baptise' pagan cult objects: we read, for instance, that in Cornwall St Sampson put the sign of the cross on a megalithic stone, thus christianizing it. The name of *Kirkja,* Old Norse for 'church', is often found in Cumbria attached to prehistoric circles and cairns, which points to an acknowledgement by the Irish Norse that they believed them to be temples and burials of former inhabitants otherwise forgotten. In Icelandic folklore, names like *Alfakirkja* and *Troiakirkja* attached to ancient stones and burials portray the folk belief that elves and trolls had their own churches. Cumbrian Vikings also may well have believed that these mysterious mounds and ruins were the homes and temples of supernatural beings. Certainly the howes were thought of as the dwellings of fairies and departed spirits.

Kirksanton, west of Millom, however, is probably called after an Irish saint, Sanctan. A parish in the Isle of Man is also so named, but the popular explanation for this is here found in the legend that a church once stood where the tarn of Kirksanton now is, until the waters rose to cover it. By an apparent miracle the church reappeared on the Isle of Man, so that, according to folk belief, Kirksanton means 'the church which sank'. Further inland, behind Black Coombe, is the fine circle of Swinside called Sunken Kirk, known at least as early as 1642 as *Chapel Sucken*. As late as 1872 it was still marked on maps as 'Druidical Temple'. Hutchinson in 1794, referring to several circles at Swinside, wrote: 'The neighbouring people call those places by the emphatical name of Sunken Kirks'.

Kirkstone Pass has recent folklore attached to it to account for its name, for in 1913 a stone was first pointed out to me as being the Kirk Stone and enquiries show that this belief still continues. The boulder stands on the left bank above the road as it descends from the summit of the pass towards Brothers Water and is about four feet high. The antiquary Machel is the first to record this particular lore of the Kirk Stone in his journal of 1692 when he wrote, 'The Kirkstone Fell takes its name from a rigid stone like the roof of a house which some have imagined (when churches were indifferent buildings without bells and steeples) to be a church'. It is interesting to recall that the early stave churches in Norway, like that still standing at Borgund-in-Sogn, were pyramidal-shaped buildings with steep roofs — like the Kirk Stone — of receding size, superimposed one on another, quite unlike the later square-towered low-roofed Norman churches. Indeed, the stave churches are believed to have resembled former Norse pagan temples. West in his *Guide to the Lakes* (1778) refers to the pass as that of High Trough and mentions 'some remarkable stones near the gorge of the pass'. Wordsworth, however supports the claim of the single stone to have given the Pass its name. In his *Ode to the Pass of Kirkstone* he described the rock,

> whose Church-like frame,
> Gives to the savage Pass its name.

The name Kirkstone was used before 1184 and a sixteenth-century document refers to the *Rayse of Kirkstone* (from the Norse *hreysi*, a cairn.) A burial, probably marked by a cairn, like that on Dunmail Raise, was found in 1840 on the site when the inn was being built. The name Kirkstone probably stems from the Irish Norse period when ancient heaps of stones were called 'kirks', while the existence of the boulder which resembles early steep-roofed Norse churches, probably provided an additional aptness for the name.

No actual remains of pagan Norse temples have been found in Cumbria but the place-names *Hoff* and *Hoff Lunn* south west of Appleby are probably from the ON *hof* 'heathen temple' and Lunn may well represent a *lund*, or 'sanctuary grove' of Viking times. A mile south-wast of Hoff, the farm house called Hofflunn stands in a wood, which may well have been the original pagan grove of the place name.

The name of the Cumbrian circle 'Meg with hir daughters, and long meg' is first found recorded by Camden. It was then regarded as a Roman monument. But the description which Camden uses was sent to him about 1600 by Reginald Bainbrigg, the earliest known Westmorland antiquary who signed himself 'scole mister of Applebie'. He wrote:

> Besides Little Salkeld . . . wher the Romaines have fought some great battle, ther standes certaine . . . pyramides of stone, placed ther in the manner of a crown. They are commonlie called meg with hir daughters. They are huge great stones, long meg standes above the ground in sight xv fote long and tre fathome about.

The original Long Meg was a noted virago of Westminster, who lived in the reign of Henry VIII. Her name was applied to objects 'of hop-pole height, wanting breadth and proportion thereto'. This revival of interest by scholars like Bainbrigg and Camden, in prehistoric monuments, did not begin to develop until after the Renaissance. During the Middle Ages interest in pagan monuments, history and literature had been frowned upon by the Church; but the revival of the study of classical writers in the fifteenth century caused an upsurge of curiosity regarding the Celts and Druids described in these Greek and Roman texts. True, Camden had recorded the Long Meg circle as a Roman monument. But after John Aubrey's visit to Avebury in 1648 he later published his conclusion that both it and Stonehenge were Druid Temples, and his hypothesis was widely accepted. When, therefore, in 1725 Dr. William Stukeley visited, measured, sketched and carefully described the Long Meg circle, he stated that it was a Celtic Temple. By 1733, Stukeley had decided that Long Meg and similar circles were Druidic, and soon a flourishing folklore was developing in England and France around the functions, rites and beliefs of this Celtic priesthood. Professor Piggott has dealt fully in his book *The Druids,* not only with the creation of Druid myth and folklore, but also with the full range of sources concerning them and with early Celtic civilisation. It is only in modern times that the great stone circles, to which Long Meg and the Keswick Carles belong, are thought to have been erected in the Bronze Age possibly for ceremonial purposes, and to have been used in some cases for burials. The smaller circles are thought to have been the ring fences for burial cairns.

But though, during the seventeenth and eighteenth centuries, scholars and antiquaries were developing their own historical and literary lore about megalithic circles, more ancient beliefs about them had long existed among country folk. Professor Jackson reminds us that one local legend about Long Meg and Her Daughters represented them as turned to stone for dancing on Sundays; another version refers to the stones as Meg's lovers, while a third recounts that if a piece of stone were broken off Long Meg, she would bleed.

A further belief that the stones of the circle, like those of the Keswick Carles and the Swinside circle, cannot be counted correctly is attached to other megalithic monuments in England, with instances in Wales and Ireland. The tradition with regard to

Long Meg was recorded by Celia Fiennes who toured the counties of England during the seventeenth century. She noted that the local people believed that the Long Meg stones 'cannot be counted twice alike, as is the story of Stonige' (Stonehenge). L. V. Grinsell adds that it was held locally that the enchantment would be broken if the stones were counted correctly or the same result was achieved twice.

The origin of the belief in uncountable stones perhaps arose from a primitive fear that numbering anything gave the one who counted power over the objects numbered, and that 'they' — the objects — might not like it. It was therefore unlucky to count or to interfere with these magic stones. Certain it is that when Colonel Lacy, who enlarged the Lacy caves on the Eden, also tried to remove the Long Meg stones by blasting, such a tempest of rain, thunder and lightning arose that the workmen fled, terrified. Fear of supernatural forces doubtless prevented any resumption of the work of destruction against Long Meg and Her Daughters.

We have seen how later populations in the Lake Counties continued to revere the sacred stones and burials of former inhabitants. They also continued to use the sacred symbols of the circle, spiral and maze of these early times, although after their conversion to Christianity, the cross was added to the pagan signs as an additional source of power and protection. The earliest known spiral and circle on a Christian grave slab to have survived in the north-west was erected at Whithorn near the abbey founded by St Ninian. Christian converts in early Britain had adopted the Roman practice of setting up inscribed slabs over the graves of their dead. Several examples of these, ranging in date from about the mid-fifth to the eighth or ninth centuries have survived in the north-west, and were discovered at or not far from Whithorn, where they can be seen in the Abbey Museum. The broken slab which bears the circle with a spiral running off to the left forms a link with early stones, like that at Glassonby in the Little Meg circle, which bears the same symbols of circle and spiral. The Whithorn stone is thought to be of the eighth century, and its interest lies in the proof it provides of the longevity of the use of the circle and spiral and how deeply rooted in a people is the belief in the power of symbols. In fact we find them repeated again in more sophisticated patterns in the wonderful series of standing stone crosses made by Anglians and Norse, in succession to engraved stone slabs as memorials to the dead.

Professor Toynbee has shown how in Roman Britain representations of pagan gods and other symbols were used at Christian places of cult and burial. Among these, Neptune, surrounded by sea-beasts, is thought to symbolise the journey of Christian souls to the Blessed Isles, while Cupids probably represented Christian spirits in paradisial bliss. In the same way, after the colonisation of Cumbria by the pagan Norse from the Isle of Man and Ireland, and subsequent to their semi-conversion to Christianity, they continued to use pagan motifs and symbols on the Christian monuments and crosses of the tenth and eleventh centuries.

On the standing cross in Dearham churchyard, Calverley has suggested that the shaft of the monument has been carved to represent the Norse sacred ash tree Yggdrasil. The fact that the roots continue carved below ground level, and that on the western face the branches pass under the rainbow bridge Bifrost, supports this suggestion. The gods had to cross Bifrost to reach the Urdar well at the foot of Yggdrasil, where they met in daily council. The cross is wheel-headed, the circle symbolizing immortality, the Sun God, also Christ, the Light of the World. The rainbow also figures in the Christian Bible as symbol of God's promise never again to drown the world.

Many other monuments in Cumbria, using motifs familiar to the Norse, from their own myths could, nevertheless, be interpreted as symbolic also of Christian beliefs. Thus, even from early times church monuments and works of art became a kind of folk Bible which could be understood by an illiterate and still semi-pagan people.

Calverley and Collingwood have suggested that the sculptor of the Gosforth cross has used motifs from a Norse poem sung, doubtless, in our district in the tenth century but not written down until later. This was the *Völuspa*, included in the *Edda* – a collection of poems about Scandinavian mythology, recorded in Iceland by Saemund Sigfusson in the thirteenth century. The *triquetra* shown on the arms of the cross – three interlaced arcs – are the Norse signs for Trinity. In the pagan period the triquetra probably represented Odin, giver of the breath of life, Haenir, bestower of sense and motion, and Lodur who imparted blood, speech, sight and hearing to living beings. On the cross shaft the dragon serpent and his progeny, symbols of evil, can be seen, while the Norse hart, the solar stag, is the symbol of the god Vidar, on this cross the prototype of Christ. Here too, is Heimdal watchman of the gods with his horn and spear, ready to confront the dragons, while the evil Loki, the bound Devil, has venom dripping from a serpent at his head which his wife, holding a basin, is trying to intercept. The crucifixion is also depicted and to the newly converted Norse the Christ, who conquered death, must have been synonymous with Baldur – the One Who Should Come to create a new heaven and earth. Indeed, the themes used on the Gosforth cross, made shortly before AD 1,000 when it was popularly believed that the world would end, must have appeared to the primitive Norse as a saga in stone conveying the hopeful messages both of the pagan *Völuspa* and of the Christian *Testament*.

Other originally pagan symbols used on Norse Christian monuments were the *triskele,* the *swastika* and the sun-snake. The *triskele* is a three-legged spiral, sign of Woden, head of the Norse Trinity. It can be seen on cross fragments at Distington and Isel. The *triquetra,* the unbroken, three-fold interlace, is again a sign of the Trinity and of eternity. It is found in the *Book of Kells* and other manuscripts of the early Christian church, and, as we have seen, on the arms of the Gosforth cross.

The *swastika,* also known as the fylfot cross and as Thor's hammer, was the sign of the Scandinavian god of Thunder. It is familiar as a Nazi symbol but it was also sacred to the Buddhists long before it was used on Christian-Norse monuments. It can be seen in our district on the 'Kenneth' shaft at Dearham. On a fragment at Aspatria it is accompanied by circles, perhaps the eternity sign or maybe representing the Holy Bread. It is also on the Isel fragment with the sun-snake, perhaps another sign of Thor, Odin, and Frey.

We come now to foundation legends and traditions regarding Cumbrian churches. The area is singularly lacking in these, but Bolton Old Church, in the upper Ellen valley north of Bassenthwaite, is said to have been built through the magic arts of Michael Scot, the wizard reputed to have died at Holm Cultram Abbey around 1291.

The church of Crosby Garrett has no tradition of magic in its actual erection but of supernatural direction as to its site. The original intention was to build it in the valley where material was deposited to this end. Its removal to the top of the hill seemed to indicate that the church should be built there, where it now stands.

Two legends of disappearing churches have already been told – the first at Kirksanton, the other concerns the predecessor of the beautiful twelfth to sixteenth-century church at Kirkby Lonsdale in Southern Cumbria.

A tradition regarding the 'lost' church of St Michael, Addingham, with its hamlet of Leigham or Adynam (Addingham) on the east bank of the Eden, was recorded by Edmund Bogg when he visited the district in 1897. He found there 'a deep-rooted tradition' that the original church of St Michael, now at Maughanby, east of Glassonby, once stood on the banks of the Eden. Bogg could find no trace of this church and concluded, that since the Long Meg circle lay only half a mile to the south, these stories of an earlier building by the river stemmed from age old traditions connected with the near-by pagan circle, described by him as 'the largest Druidical temple in Britain'. The church at Maughanby has the fragment of an early ninth century cross and also a wheel-headed cross with a section of the shaft made about the eleventh century, standing in the churchyard. It was not until 1912 that the vicar discovered that the wheel-headed cross had been brought during the previous century by the great uncle of a 77-year-old parishioner from the banks of the Eden and placed on his family grave in the churchyard at Maughanby. This confirms Jefferson's statement that the cross had originally come from the old chapel by the Eden. Until 1913, however, it was still thought that the present church of St Michael had stood there from early times and that it was a building known as the Chapel of Salkeld which had stood at Kirk Bank by the Eden, with the hamlet clustering round it and known as Leigham or Adynam (Addingham). In the summer of 1913 a prolonged drought made it possible to inspect the river bed into which the old church had collapsed in the time of some great flood. A broken hog back, a rude standing stone with a cross, the base of a cross, marked out for the game, Nine Mens Morris and a broken Norman grave slab were recovered from the river and placed in St Michael's church at Maughanby, and the tradition which Bogg collected about the original old church was proved right. St Michael's well can still be found, but it is now on the west bank of the river which during the flood undermined the 60-foot eastern bank. It fell, carrying with it the churchyard, the long abandoned and ruined church of St Michael and cottages of the hamlet of Leigham or Adynam.

A few other church legends concern bells. That of Great Salkeld, with a fortified tower, is reputed to have been built by Dick Whittington, traditionally believed to have been born in the Parish. He is said to have had three large bells made for the church which were, however, retained at Kirkby Stephen.

The bell and steeple of Blawith church, south of Coniston are commemorated in a doggerel rhyme:

> Blawith poor people,
> An old church
> And new steeple,
> As poor as Hell
> They had to sell
> A bit of fell
> To buy a bell,
> Blawith poor people.

Near Boot in Eskdale is the typical dale chapel of St Catherine with her well – now disused – near-by. The bell bears her name and is traditionally believed to have hung on a tree on the neighbouring Bell's Hill, so that the chimes would carry further up and down the valley.

St Michael's church at Bowness on Solway has two bells in the porch which link us with the Scottish Wars. Raiders are said to have crossed the Firth and to have returned towards Scotland carrying the two bells of St Michael's with them. They were pursued so hotly by the Cumberland men that they had to drop the bells in the Solway at a place still called the Bell Pool. On a return raid the English Borderers carried off two Scottish bells – still in the porch of Bowness church, perhaps an indication of belief in 'an eye for an eye'.

A final tradition concerns a helmet and sword which hang on the wall of the outer north aisle of the fine old parish church at Kendal. They are said to have belonged to Robin the Devil, a member of the Philipson family which supported Charles I in the Civil War. Robin had been besieged in his brother's house on Long Holme, now Belle Isle, in Windermere, by Colonel Briggs, a Roundhead officer, but was finally relieved by his brother. The story of Robin's attempted revenge against Colonel Briggs in Kendal Church was first recorded by the Reverend Thomas Machel in the journal which he kept of several tours on horseback around the Barony of Kendal between October 1691 and March 1693. The account was written within 50 years of the events described. Machel writes:

> The next day being Sunday, Mr Robert Philipson with three or four more rode to Kendal to take revenge of the committee men [Briggs and his supporters]. He passed the watch and rode into the church, up one aisle and down another to sacrifice; one of them met him, whom I shall not name, but he was dehorsed in his return by the guards, and his girths broke, but his partners relieved him by a desperate charge, and Robin in a trice clapped his saddle on horse-back and vaulted on him without girth or stirrup, killed a sentinel and galloped away returning to the island by two o'clock. Upon this and suchlike adventures he was commonly called 'Robin the Divil', but he was killed at last in the Irish wars at Washford fight as is reported.

This story is repeated almost verbatim in 1777 by Nicolson and Burn and by Clarke in his *Survey of the Lakes* in 1789. In neither work is Robin's helmet or sword mentioned. By 1861, however, Cornelius Nicholson in his *Annals of Kendal* tells us that 'a popular narrative had grown up around the helmet, by then hanging in Kendal church'; it was then known as 'the Rebel's Cap'. Nicolson points out that the helmet was in 1861 suspended over Sir Roger Bellingham's tomb in the church and concluded that it had belonged to that knight banneret. He then proceeds to recount the 'popular narrative' broadly following Machel's account but adding that:

> in passing out at one of the upper doors, Robin's head struck against the portal, when his helmet, unclasped by the blow, fell to the ground and was retained .... The helmet was afterwards hung aloft as a commemorating badge of sacrilegious temerity. This narrative is still extant in a ballad of the times entitled, 'Dick and the Devil', now of course extremely rare. The adventure is celebrated also by Scott in his poem of Rokeby.

In 1900, in Curwen's *Kirkbie Kendall,* we are told that a sword hanging near the Rebel's Cap was 'a modern addition', and on a previous page we learn that in 1863 Mr John Broadbent, a descendant of the Bellinghams, had caused the lost brasses to be replaced by modern ones on the Bellingham tomb and also had a sword which he had bought in London hung over it alongside the Rebel's Cap. Mr Titus Wilson, the proprietor of the charming old shop in Kendal Highgate which still bears his name, is reported to have been with Mr. Broadbent when the sword was hung over the tomb.

In conclusion, the story as told by Machel is undoubtedly authentic, especially as he records that the Rector of Windermere was one of his informers, with whom he lodged for the night in the old Rectory still standing in Bowness. Moreover the Rector William Wilson born about 1530 was the son of Thomas Wilson of Kendal, who could well have been present when Robin Philipson rode into the church in search of his enemy. Indeed the Parson himself could have witnessed the affray as a small boy. Machel also tells us that Sir Christopher Philipson, Robin's uncle, was his informant in Windermere. It should be noted that the story was retold without additions for about 200 years. By 1861, although Nicolson believed that the helmet was Sir Roger Bellingham's, it was already known in popular tradition as the Rebel's Cap, and was regarded as having belonged to Robin the Devil, whose dashing exploits had fired popular imagination. The hanging of the sword in 1863 was known only to a few, and since it was placed near the helmet, has been drawn into the lore surrounding Robin the Devil, by those ignorant of its reputed purchase in 1863.

The Lucks of
Cumbria

ONE OF THE outstanding features of Cumbrian folklore concerns the idea of luck. There are at least six ancient houses or families in Cumberland which still, or until recent times, possessed a relic which was regarded as safeguarding the luck of the dwelling which housed it and of the owners who guarded it – providing that the object called the 'Luck' was cherished and remained unbroken.

The most ancient and also the most famous of these Lucks is that of Edenhall, a parish near Penrith. This is a glass vase enamelled in red, blue, green, white and gilt. Of Syrian manufacture, it is thought to have been made in Aleppo during the thirteenth century when that town was famous for glass-making. This was the period of the First Crusade so that the Luck was probably brought back to England by a returning Crusader. The story told about the origin of the Luck, however, ascribes it to the fairies who lived in or near St Cuthbert's well, still to be seen in the garden of the mansion of Edenhall, now demolished. The butler of the Musgraves, who then owned the hall, went to the well for water and surprised a company of fairies dancing round the goblet. He seized it. Unable to retrieve their treasure, the small folk disappeared, singing:

> If that glass should break or fall
> Farewell the luck of Edenhall.

Today many people in the district believe that the glass was broken and that as a result the Musgrave family died out and their hall was demolished. But the Luck was unharmed and is one of the treasures in the Victoria and Albert Museum. Its embossed case of *cuir bouilli* (boiled leather), specially made to hold the glass in the fourteenth century, is also housed there. This case bears the sacred monogram I.H.S. – the initials of Jesus' name in Greek – suggesting that the chalice may have held the sacrificial wine during Mass in the family chapel at Edenhall or in St Cuthbert's ancient church nearby.

The first literary mention of the Luck was in 1729 in James Ralph's recension of the 'Wharton ballad' where the poet changed the opening lines of the original to

> God prosper long from being broke
> The Luck of Edenhall.

Sir William Musgrave, member of a collateral branch of the family-owners of Edenhall since the fifteenth century, wrote the first circumstantial account of the Luck. This appeared in the *Gentleman's Magazine* of 1791. He mentions St Cuthbert's Well, thus linking the legend of the vase to the medieval cult of that saint, which suggests that the local traditions surrounding the relic were of long standing. Moreover, Edenhall lies on the route supposedly taken by the monks who carried the saint's body, seeking safety for it from Danish raids, and Edenhall church is dedicated to St Cuthbert.

Sir William also states that the leather case was the second to have housed the glass. This appears likely, for covers sold in the east for such goblets were of wood.

A similar glass to that of Edenhall was the 'Goblet of the Eight Priests' bequeathed to the Cathedral of Douai in 1329 by Marguerite Mullet or Mallet. The significant fact about this is that the priests drank annually from the cup each year in remembrance of their benefactress. Another chalice in the Isle of Man — so closely linked in the past with Cumbria — throws further light on the probable function of these Lucks. This was a bell-shaped crystal tumbler decorated with floral scrolls and pillars on two sides. The glass belonged to the Fletchers of Ballafletcher until at least 1678. A century later it was sold and later given to Colonel Wilkes, who bought the Ballafletcher estate; the donors probably thought that the talisman should belong to the owner of the house, since tradition said that it had been given to a Fletcher with the injunction 'that as long as he preserved it, peace and plenty would follow, but woe to him who broke it as he would surely be haunted by the *lhiannan Shee* or "peaceful spirit" of Ballafletcher'. The goblet was therefore carefully preserved, but at Christmas it was 'filled with wine and quaffed off at a breath by the head of the house only, as libation to the spirit for her protection'. This glass, unfortunately can no longer be traced.

Here again in the Island, colonized, like Cumbria, by the Norse, is found the female guardian spirit who, as portrayed in the saga, bestowed peace and plenty on the house and family she guarded. Originally this spirit was believed to live on after the death of the man she favoured, but to him was granted the power of passing on his 'luck' to another, usually to one of his own family. A vessel therefore dedicated for use in pagan ceremonies to the guardian spirit would come to be regarded as sacred in its own right. Then, through transference, would be thought of as containing the Luck of the person or house as long as the object remained unbroken. Dr Hartland suggests that the Luck of Edenhall was originally such a sacrificial goblet dedicated to this old pagan worship of the guardian or house spirits. The policy of the church was to baptize to Christian uses as many of these pagan objects, beliefs and ceremonies as possible. Perhaps when the new cover was made for the Luck of Edenhall in the fourteenth century the sacred letters of Jesus' name were engraved on it, to christianize this former fairy and therefore pagan goblet. The same idea is illustrated by the fact that pagan Norse who drank to Odin, when converted, pledged instead Our Lord and His Apostles. Indeed in *Njal's Saga* the Norseman Hallr only consented to be baptized if St Michael undertook to be his guardian spirit. The tradition regarding the Luck of Edenhall with its pagan, fairy origin and its christianized cover, fits in, therefore, with the accounts of several chalices in Sweden said to have been gifts from Berg-women. These vessels were later dedicated to the service of the church in order to annul their pagan origin. Indeed it was suggested in the early eighteenth century that the Luck served for some time as a chalice, and considering that the case was 'christianized' in the fourteenth century — the period of the Scottish Wars — it may have been thought that a crystal glass was less likely to be carried off by raiders than a silver goblet. It is interesting that a tenth-century canon permitted glass chalices to be used instead of silver, though wooden vessels were forbidden.

Finally, Dr Hartland points out that the theme of cups stolen from the fairies is found only in stories and traditions of Teutonic and Scandinavian races, and authentic records of the preservation of such treasures belong only to houses in districts where these people settled and where heathen rites lingered longest, owing to their inhabitants' late conversion to Christianity.

Although the Luck no longer belongs to the Musgrave family and their house, whose fortunes it was thought to guard no longer, alas, exists, in Edenhall village the fairy glass is still talked of with affection and a certain awe. Miss Graham and her cousin, Mrs. Towler, still live in Rose Cottage, once their grandparents' home, opposite the hall. Mr Davidson was clerk of works to the Musgraves and both recall being told by him that Lady Musgrave asked him to make a special box to hold the Luck and its leather case. This he did, and Mr Davidson placed the glass and its box for safety beneath his bed. To recall that — even if only for one night — the famous Luck actually rested beneath their roof, gives his granddaughters the greatest pleasure. Next day Mr Davidson sadly took the glass in its special box to place it on the train at Penrith for its journey to London. Now, whenever Miss Graham and her cousin go there, they always make a special journey to the Victoria and Albert Museum to visit 'our Luck'. Was the sad end of the saga inevitable, they wonder, once the Luck — symbol of the guardian spirit — was exiled from the hall it was believed to guard?

Another Cumbrian Luck with a somewhat different origin is the fifteenth-century glass basin preserved in Muncaster Castle, near Ravenglass. Seven inches in diameter and decorated with white enamel mouldings, this was presented to Sir John Pennington by King Henry VI when he was given refuge at the Castle after the

Lancastrian defeat at Hexham in 1463. It is said that Henry had been refused admission at Irton Hall. Shepherds found him wandering on the fell and took him to the Castle. In Muncaster Church is a stone which records: 'Holie Kinge Harrye gave Sir John a brauce wrkyd glass cuppe . . . whylles the familie shold keep hit unbrecken they shold gretely thryve.' The cup, *unbrecken,* is still treasured at Muncaster and descendants of the Penningtons still thrive there. Though never owned by fairies, the King, donor of the gift, is described as *Holie* and was believed to be imbued with supernatural power sufficient to give protection and blessing to its recipients. This power was regarded as being symbolized by the unbroken Luck itself.

The Luck of Burrell Green, still treasured on the farm of that name in the parish of Great Salkeld, is a brass dish about $16\frac{1}{4}$ inches in diameter with a central boss decorated with a version of the voluted rose. It formerly had the words, 'Mary, Mother of Jesus, Saviour of Men', engraved round the boss in late Gothic letters. In more recent lettering, in the outer circle, there appeared:

> If this dish be sold or gi'en,
> Farewell the Luck of Burrell Green.

Continuous cleaning of the dish has almost worn away the words.

The earliest printed reference to this Luck appears to be in L. P. White's *Lore of the Lake Counties* published in 1873. Perhaps the latest account — by a former member of the Lamb family who had bought Burrell Green — comes from a letter written by Mrs. G. Rycroft of Tasmania in December 1959 to the Armstrongs, tenants of Colonel Thompson, owner of Burrell Green. She states that she was told the story of the Luck by her father when she was a child; that the date of the dish is about 1417, and that it was given at a wedding feast held in the house when a Lamb daughter married a King of Mardale. A servant went to the well for water where some hob-goblins appeared and said, 'Bring us food and wine and we'll bless the wedding'. The servant complied and was given the dish. Mr Lamb, in a paper read in 1897, implied that the dish had occult powers, since it fell down three times in succession when the farm changed owners.

The present house took its name from John Burrell who either built or rebuilt it in the early seventeenth century. There is also a Burrell Green of the same period in Penrith. Was the Luck in John Burrell's possession then? Like the Luck of Edenhall, its true origin is likely to remain a mystery. Nevertheless, the antecedents in Celtic myth of such 'a wide and deep platter' like that at Burrell Green are interesting. The Irish sagas have as a recurring theme that of the mortal hero entertained in a supernatural palace, where a sumptuous feast was provided, according to his wishes, in a lordly dish, together with unlimited wine held in a magic horn. The cup or horn and the platter (*graal*) were in fact pagan symbols of plenty, and stories concerning them were recited in Wales and Cumbria by travelling Irish bards in the Middle Ages and were carried by Bretons to France and to the Anglo-Normans. A Welsh list of the *Thirteen Treasures of Britain* includes the *dysgl*, or platter of Rhydderch, the historic sixth-century king of Strathclyde and Cumbria. The prototype of the original owner of the magic platter was probably the British god Bran, son of Llyr. By a mistaken translation the word *graal* was taken to mean a cup or chalice and so passed into the Grail legend as the cup from which Christ drank. Some writers, however, including the twelfth-century Chrétien de Troyes, recognized the *graal* as the 'wide and deep platter' mentioned above, from which Christ took meat at the Passover supper with His disciples.

The fifteenth-century platter of Burrell Green also belongs in date to the period when European drinking horns were inscribed with the Virgin's name and with those of the Three Kings of Cologne. This linked them with the Feast of Christmas. The name of the Virgin on the Luck of Burrell Green, together with the couplet concerning the Luck, also links it to the Manx Luck of Ballafletcher in which, during that festival, a toast was drunk to the house spirit; the shape of the dish resembles that of the Celtic platter of plenty as well as to that traditionally associated with the Last Supper. This union of pagan and Christian symbolism is far from uncommon. Finally, just as some European horns were reputed to have been gifts from Berg women or trolls and were handed over to the use of the Church to be christianized, so the platter of Burrell Green was said to be the gift of a Hob, and the engraving of the Virgin's name upon it is paralleled by the addition of the sacred monogram to the leather cover of the fairy goblet of Edenhall.

The Luck of Workington follows next in date. This was the gift of Mary Queen of Scots to Sir Henry Curwen who entertained her at Workington Hall on her first night of exile in England on 16 May 1568, after her defeat at Langside. This Luck is an agate cup, which Lord Herries had brought from Dundrennan Abbey in the hastily packed basket of provisions for the queen's flight across the Solway to England. The goblet is still in the possession of Mr E. S. C. Curwen of Belle Isle, Windermere, and can be seen there on display in the beautiful Georgian Round House on the island. Like the Luck of Muncaster, it was the gift of a sovereign commonly believed to rule by Divine Right. Moreover, both Mary and 'Holie Kinge Harrye' were, after their tragic deaths, regarded by many as martyrs and as such, imbued with supernatural power – though of a different order from that of fairies and hobs – to bestow blessing and plenty. This was symbolized by their gifts which, in both cases, took the form of a drinking vessel.

Two other Lucks, one connected with Haresceugh Castle, near Renwick, of which only the site remains, and one belonging to the farm at Nether Haresceugh, are not well known. The former, a wooden bowl with a silver rim, has vanished. Apparently a couplet was engraved on the mount:

> Should this bowl fall in feast or wassail,
> Farewell the Luck of Haresceugh Castle.

Here the name *Haresceugh* contains *skogr,* the old Norse for *wood;* here, also, the Norse idea of Luck as a guardian spirit symbolized by a drinking vessel is preserved.

Nether Haresceugh, like the site of the castle, is in the Penrith district. Its Luck is referred to in *Our Cumberland Village* by Colonel T. Fetherstonehaugh, which is a history of Kirkoswald. This glass bowl is a deep claret colour and has a white rim. It is no longer kept at the farm, which somewhat detracts from the traditional idea that Lucks were symbolic of the guardian spirit of the house and as such should remain in the building.

There are two more recent examples of Cumbrian Lucks. The first, from Skirsgill Hall, is 'a large armorial goblet with drawn trumpet bowl and plain stem containing an elongated tear'. The bowl is engraved with the words 'The Luck of Skirsgill, September

1st, Anno 1732'. A tulip decorates one side, and a fruiting vine the other. The arms of Whelpdale of Skirsgill are engraved between. This glass was probably made to commemorate the betrothal of William Whelpdale and Mary, daughter of John Brougham. The two were married at Dacre on 21 December 1732. Some 230 years later, the Luck was sold at Sothebys on 22 January 1968 by a lady whose name was not divulged. Messrs Sotheby kindly informed me that the glass was bought by Lloyds Antiques of London SW1, who have not replied to my enquiries regarding the present whereabouts of this Luck.

The second eighteenth-century Luck is that of Rydal Hall. It is mentioned in the will of Sir William Fleming made in 1736 and again demonstrates the belief that the Luck of a family will continue, provided the symbol of that luck is safely kept. Sir William's bequest is

> a pretty large gilt silver bowl with the Fleming coat of arms upon it, given by my great great grandmother (an extraordinary woman) to the heirs male of the family, to be kept by them as an heirloom and *a lucky piece of plate,* as I have reason to believe it hath been to all those who have had the keeping of it since her death.

The pagan Norse idea of luck as an attribute which could be conveyed from one person to another is still operative in a somewhat changed form among Lakeland farmers, where the luck of one man with his cattle is symbolically transferred to the purchaser of those cattle by the vendor's return to him of a portion of the purchase price. Indeed, stories are still told of the death of animals after a sale where this sum, known as Luck Money, had not been returned to the purchaser.

Customs like the return of a penny by the recipient of the gift of any cutting instrument to its donor are still prevalent in Cumbria, as elsewhere. This coin symbolises continuance of friendship after the bestowal of what could prove, under certain circumstances, a lethal gift. Perhaps originally the coin was a sort of luck offering to the guardian spirit for the continuance of a good relationship between both men, just as a coin placed in a wishing-well was a gift to the spirit of the well, so that she would ensure fulfilment of the wish, or a continuance of luck. In Coventina's Well on the Roman Wall in Cumbria, innumerable early coins were found, which demonstrated the ancient origin of this custom.

A Women's Institute member from Bampton, near Haweswater, has recorded another Luck custom. When a tenant is leaving a farm in that district, he leaves a pinch of salt on a plate to bring luck to the new, in-going tenant. It was believed that salt was hated by the Devil, witches and evil fairies.

―∽ 6 ∽―

Nature
Lore

'With rowan tree well fenced about
We're safe from every evil'

THIS OLD couplet expresses the ancient pagan belief that certain
trees were imbued with supernatural powers. Indeed, every tree was
believed to have its own indwelling spirit or dryad — from the
Greek *dpus,* a forest tree. The rowan or mountain ash sacred to the
gods of the ancient Gaels in Ireland, who ate its berries, was
believed to have power over witches and evil spirits, so that a
branch was hung in Cumbrian shippons and stables to ensure
protection for the animals within. In 1897, H. S. Cowper recorded
that a sprig of rowan was sometimes placed with the cream in the
churn 'to make the butter come'.

After the influx of the Irish-Norse into our district the common
ash must have been regarded with particular veneration, since their
sacred tree was Yggdrasil, the World Ash.

The yew tree, so often grown in churchyards, was associated in

Cumbria with the dead light, which, it was claimed, sometimes was seen as the spirit passed from the body at the moment of death. My husband, who did not particularly believe in portents, related that in 1910, when his grandmother, to whom he was devoted, died, he saw a bright round globe of light hover for some seconds over the foot of his bed about 9 o'clock, after he had put out his lamp. He was told the next morning that his grandmother had died just before 9 p.m. and that it was her dead light which he had seen. It was claimed that this was often seen by mourners at funerals. The Rev. H. J. Bulkley also recorded in 1886 that in Bewcastle it was believed possible, but risky, to see the spirit form of the recently buried by watching in the churchyard at night. For this, a long branch of yew had to be cut with a wide, V-shaped notch at the end. The branch had to be held in the left hand, together with the knife. The end of the branch rested on the ground, while the watcher, kneeling on his left knee, supported his right elbow on his right knee and with his right hand firmly closed his right eye, then by peering beyond the notch and open knife it was said that he would see the spirit of the dead light. One bold youth fulfilled all the conditions and reported that he actually saw a dead light approaching in the dark, but jumped up in 'sic a fright' to flee from the apparition that he injured his left eye.

Another old man of the same district used to cut yew into weird shapes to give the pieces to his friends, claiming that these would protect them from the six evils. Unfortunately the vicar's informant could not remember further details. It may be recalled, however, that 'slips of yew, silvered in the moon's eclipse' were included in their noxious brew by the witches in *Macbeth*.

In 1895, W. G. Collingwood recorded the dressing on Maundy Thursday of a great oak tree which overhung the fountain at Satterthwaite. Coloured rags and crockery were hung on the branches and a similar ceremony took place at Hawkshead Hill that year. This custom was a survival of ancient tree and well worship and showed that conversion to the Christian faith had not eradicated the old customs, although the wells had been re-dedicated to the saints.

Perhaps the most interesting tree lore belongs to the hazel bush, though its origins and meaning are obscure. In Scandinavian and German mythology this tree held an important place, and in modern times the forked hazel twig is still regarded as the most potent aid in water divining. The straight handle of a forked branch is held in the right hand of the outstretched arm as the 'dowser' walks over the ground to be tested. The fork twists and dips as it passes over hidden water – that is if the diviner himself possesses the necessary power.

Burials with hazel wands and leaves belonging to widely separated periods have been found, not only in Cumbria, but in cemeteries as far afield as Swabia. During the restoration of Dearham church, the uncoffined skeleton of a man was found resting on a bed of ivy and hazel leaves, while a cross made from two hazel wands had been placed on his body. Alongside was another burial, in this case in a coffin which had been placed on two hazel wands in the form of a St Andrew's cross. Similar hazel wands have been found in Anglian burials at Selby, in St Richard's tomb at Chichester (1253), at Hereford, in Bishop Mayo's grave (1516), and also in Alemannic tree coffins at Oberflacht in Swabia. This last burial sugggests a pagan origin for the custom; possibly it stemmed from the German belief in the hazel worm which took the form of a crowned white snake which lived beneath the hazel tree. The snake is traditionally symbolic of wisdom and subtlety while the crown denotes sovereignty.

In the Scandinavian *Eigils Saga* a trial is described in which the judges were fenced in by hazel staves joined by ropes-*vébond*. Originally *vé* was Scandinavian for 'sanctuary', which conveys the idea here that justice was originally administered by priests, or a priest-king, representative on earth of the gods. So that in both German and Scandinavian tradition, as indeed in modern use, the hazel is associated with ideas of justice, wisdom, sovereignty and divination. Possibly, therefore, hazel wands and crosses found in early graves indicated that their occupants, if formerly pagan, were priest diviners, and if Christian, as in the case of St Richard and Bishop Mayo, that they held priestly authority, and exercized jurisdiction in their dioceses and in the ecclesiastical courts.

Calverley has another suggestion drawn from the floriated St Andrew's cross on the 'Adam' stone at Dearham. He thinks that the hazel wands in the nearby graves may be connected with a legend about St Kentigern, one of the early missionaries to Cumbria. The saint had found that his monastery fires had been maliciously

extinguished. He thereupon broke off a green hazel bough, prayed
to the Trinity, and blew upon it. Immediately the twigs burst into
flame enabling the saint to relight his altar candles, and monastery
fires.

The White Thorn, May Tree or Hawthorn was also traditionally
associated in Lakeland with places of trial and courts of justice. Two
places remain where a young thorn tree still marks the site where
courts were once held. The first, near Hesket-in-the-Forest, we have
already mentioned as having been seen by Hutchinson: an earlier
tree marked the place where tenants of Inglewood held their Court
of the Forest. A young tree was planted some years ago to grow
through a hole in a wayside platform on the site where the original
Court Thorn once flourished. It is mentioned in the *Awntyres off
Arthure,* written about 1450-70 in connection with Tarn Wadling,
referred to there as 'the tarn with the flourishing thorn'. The other
Court Thorn was stated by Collingwood to have been east of the
village and west of the bridge at Anthorn on the north shore of
Moricambe Bay, Solway Firth. Here also a local court used to be
held.

It is still believed in Cumbria, as elsewhere, that the bringing of
May blossom into a house will be followed by a death or news of a
death. Like the rowan, the hawthorn is associated with the ancient
divine dynasty of Ireland, and May Day, called Beltane, was an
important Celtic festival. May blossom was hung on the
outside of houses to celebrate this day when the Celtic sun festival
was held. Uncanny happenings were often known to occur on May
Eve and May Day.

A traditional rhyme, still well known, refers perhaps to the
month of May, or more logically to the blossom:

Don't cast a clout, Till May be out.

If the blossom flowers early, the weather will be warm enough for
clothing to be discarded, but not otherwise. This dictum is still
followed, at least by more elderly Cumbrians.

We come now to trees in Cumbria with traditional associations
and legends. One of these, the Hartshorn Tree, seems to have first
been recorded by Lady Anne Clifford in her *Memoirs* in 1658.
There she wrote:

This summer, by some few mischievous people secretly in the night, there was broken off and taken down from that tree, neare the paile of Whinfield Parke (which for that cause was called the Hart's Horne Tree) one of those old Hart's Horns which (as is mentioned in the summerie of my Ancestors, Robert Lord Clifford's Life) was sett upp in the year 1333 att a general huntinge, when Edward Ballioll, then King of Scots . . . lay for a while in the said Lord Clifford's castle in Westmorland, where the King hunted a greate stag which was killed neare the said Oak Tree. In memory whereof the hornes were nayled up in it, growing as it were naturally in the Tree, and have remained there ever since, till in 1648 one of those Hornes was broken down by some of the Army and the other was broken down as aforsaid this yeare. So, as there is no part thereof remayning, the Tree itself being now so decayed . . . that it cannot last long.

The story is that a hound Hercules chased the stag from Whinfell to Redkirks in Scotland and back. On reaching the park the stag leapt the fence, but died on the far side; Hercules tried to follow but fell back and also expired. This took place near Hornby Hall, not far from Ninekirks Church, and a folk rhyme commemorates the event,

> Hercules killed Hart-a grees,
> Hart-a grees killed Hercules.

Lady Anne, however, in 1670 stopped her coach between Appleby and Brougham to gaze once more on the tree which, probably to her surprise, was still defying the ravages of time, 12 years after her prophecy of its approaching end.

In 1731 Sir James Clarke, a Scottish baronet, journeyed to Lowther to see his son who was at school there. He toured the district and kept a journal of his travels. In this he described a visit to the Earl of Thanet's hunting lodge in Whinfell Forest where he was shown a pair of large stag's horns which had been 'got in the heart of an oak tree, together with two clasps of iron with which they had been fixed'. He then relates the story of Hercules and Hart of Grace (sic) and concludes that 'from the evidence of the iron clasps fixed to the horns, the tradition regarding their having been fastened to an oak tree seemed not ill-founded'.

Since we know, however, of Lady Anne's assertion about the horns that in 1658 'there is no part thereof remaining', we cannot accept that the pair viewed by Sir James in 1731 were the originals which had been secured to the Harts Horn Tree in 1333. The trunk itself was still in position over a century later when it was described by Wordsworth as imposing, even in its ruined state. Nicolson and Burn repeat the story of the hunt but suggest that it went no further than round by Ninekirks, F. H. Parker, however, in 1910 argues convincingly that the tale is by no means improbable, while Dr Williamson assures us that the trunk of the old tree still existed in 1790, that the roots were *in situ* in 1807, and that in 1922 Lord Hothfield had a portion of them on his writing table in Appleby Castle.

The other tree, the Capon Tree, which arouses interest in the folklore which grew up around it — like the Hartshorn — no longer exists, but a graceful memorial marks its site near Brampton. This is on the side of the vanished old paved road from Newcastle to Carlisle at its junction with the track known as Sandy Lonning. Hutchinson suggested that the name 'Capon' arose from the custom of the judge and his retinue, en route from Newcastle to Carlisle, stopping beneath the tree to eat their provisions of capons and bread. But this explanation would not fit the other known Capon Trees at Caldbeck, one near Alnwick Castle, and another close to Ferniehurst Castle near Jedburgh. George Tate in his *History of Alnwick* relates that a ball game used to be played there under the local Capon Tree to the accompaniment of a traditional song:

> Keppy ball, Keppy ball, Coban Tree
> Come down the long lonning and tell to me,
> The form and features the speech and degree
> Of the man that is my true love to be.
> Once a maiden, two a wife,
> Three a maiden, four a wife.

The chorus was continued as long as the player caught the ball when it rebounded from the tree.

Henry Penfold refers to *capon*, *coban*, and *covin* as being the name given to any tree which stood before a Scottish mansion house under which the laird always went out to greet his visitors. From this it may be deduced that the title 'Covin Tree' may spring from *covyne*, a trysting or meeting place. Regarding the Jedburgh Capon Tree, J. C. Loudon states it was thought to be where the Border clans used to meet, the name being derived from the Scottish word *kep*, to meet. Penfold refers to the Anglo-Saxon *cepan*, to take, hold, catch, keep. From the old ball rhyme and the other derivative meanings the name points to the tree as a trysting place. This conclusion is strengthened by the testimony of William Barker of Brampton who, in 1903, told Penfold that on market days it was customary for any man who had a quarrel to settle, to shake the bull ring in the market place and to challenge his opponent to meet him under the Capon Tree, where disputes were traditionally settled in a fight.

The Capon Tree at Brampton, if originally used as a playground by children and a trysting place by lovers, was abandoned for these purposes after six of the Jacobite rebels were hanged from its branches in 1746. Prince Charles had made Brampton his headquarters for a time on his advance south. The local victims were not only hanged on the Tree but drawn and quartered, and the horrors of the execution lingered long in local memory, so that the tree was later regarded with dread as a haunted place. The decayed trunk was still a fine specimen in 1833, and as late as 1903 it is recorded that Brampton mothers often threatened their disobedient children with the Capon Tree boggles.

Some weather lore has been associated with trees and plants. A well-known couplet foretells the amount of rain to be expected:

> The oak before the ash
> Then we'll have a splash,
> The ash before the oak,
> Then we'll have a soak.

Protection against thunder and lightning was believed in Cumbria to be ensured by growing the house-leek on walls and roofs.

The belief that when blackberries have been frosted they become Devil's Fruit and are no longer fit for human consumption is still held locally. The same tradition is found in Ireland, where after Michaelmas Day it was said that the Devil had put his foot on the blackberries.

Other predictions or beliefs regarding weather are made from observation of natural features, as for instance:

> When Skiddaw fell puts on a cap,
> Criffel hill begins to drap.

With regard to the heavy rainfall experienced Under Skiddaw, near Keswick a local saying has arisen, 'If it rains we mun dee as they dee under Skiddaw'. The answer to the question,' What mun ye dee?' is, 'Ye mun let it drap'.

Another couplet concerns St Bees Head:

> St Bega's head seen fair and clear,
> Is a sign of western breezes here.

Indeed, to see the distant fells very clearly is also a bad sign. In Langdale, when rainfall is particularly heavy, the dalesfolk have a saying, 'We'll hev to borrow Langden lid'. This supposedly originated when an old statesman in the dale was asked by 'an off-comer', 'How can you stand all this rain?' 'No sa weel', he replied, 'but we're thinking on getting a lid for t'dale.'

When, in Heversham and Beetham the people hear Levens Force on the Kent which lies to the north, they expect fair weather; but when they hear the waterfall on the Bela River from the south they prepare for rain. In Fuller's edition of Camden these facts have been noted: 'On the Kent are two waterfalls, whereof the northern sounding clear and loud betokeneth fair weather; the southern, on the same terms, presageth rain.' Dr Burn points out that one of these falls is on the Bela.

A similar type of forecast was made in Kirkby Lonsdale during my childhood. We were told that gun practice in Morecambe actually brought rain to the town whereas the sound of gunfire was carried from Morecambe, which lay to the south-west, by the prevailing wind which usually brought in rain from the sea.

Brough Hill Fair, held on 1 October, has a reputation for bad weather, so that a spell of tempest and rain is often referred to in Cumbria as 'proper Brough Hill weather'. One maid, when I was a child and had a cold, used to sometimes tell me to 'stop broughing and coughing'. Was this expression derived from some devious association of the Brough Hill type of weather with colds?

A certain number of weather predictions are common in Cumbria. Fine weather can be expected when cows move to the tops of hills. Rain before seven, fine before eleven. Enough blue in the sky to make a Dutchman's (or sailor's) trousers forecasts that clouds will scatter:

Red sky at night, shepherds' delight.
Red sky at morning, shepherds' warning

Birds flying low near the ground and wind lifting the underside of leaves on trees usually foretell rain. 'As the day lengthens, the cold strengthens' is usually proved true by much colder weather after Christmas.

On St Swithin's Day (15 July) the weather was always anxiously noted during my childhood. If rain fell then it was believed that it would rain for the 40 days after. Brewer explains this tradition from the wish of St Swithin, Bishop of Winchester (died 862), to be buried in the churchyard that 'the sweet rain of heaven might water his grave'. The monks on his canonisation had planned to move his body into the choir. Such heavy rain fell, however, on the day appointed and for forty days after, that they regarded the downpour as a sign that the saint wished his body to rest in peace.

A considerable number of legends are still told concerning the wild animals which once existed in large numbers in the Lake District. Two areas claim the distinction of being the arena where the Last Wolf was slain. One of these is near the farm named *Wolfa* near Great Salkeld. The other last wolf is reputed to have been killed at the end of an arduous chase on the shore at Humphrey Head near Grange-over-Sands. The story is told in a ballad of doubtful origin in Stockdale's *Annals of Cartmel* which gives a romantic version of the tale but lacks authentic details of period or character. John, son of Sir Edgar Harrington, lord of the neighbouring manor of Wraysholm, had secretly plighted his troth to Adela, his father's ward, and had been disinherited in consequence. John joined the Crusades but some years later returned in secret, as a knight to his father's home to find a feast in progress. A wolf had been ravaging the Cartmel district and Sir Edgar had proclaimed that he would give to any unmarried knight who slew the monster his ward's hand in marriage and half the Wraysholme estates. Next day, after a gruelling chase Sir John slew the beast thereby regaining his father's love as well as the hand and heart of his former plighted bride.

A prose version of the ballad was written by Mrs Jerome Mercier under the title *The Last Wolf*. The ballad is included in this small volume together with charming illustrations, among them an old photograph of the building in which the Holy Well at Humphrey Head – mentioned in the ballad – was once housed. Early this century this was demolished, but a small shelter with a door, which was kept locked, protected the well. The key was obtainable on payment of 3d. from the neighbouring farm. This shelter was in turn destroyed after a Spa Company abandoned its project of selling the medicinal waters in Morecambe. Now, the well is sadly neglected and its brown tinted waters seep from the foot of the cliff into the pebbles of the shore. Although a younger branch of the Harringtons of Gleaston Castle in Furness was seated at Wraysholme Tower from the 13th century, there is no record of a Sir Edgar having held the manor. After certain Harringtons fought in 1487 at Stoke-by-Newark for Lambert Simnel against Henry VII, their lands were given to the Stanleys. Nevertheless, the tradition of the Harrington's connection with the story of the slaying of the Last Wolf so near to Wraysholme gains support from the place name Ulpha belonging to a farm and pool near Meathop, some three miles north east along the coast beyond Humphrey Head. According to the *Place-Names of Westmorland*, Ulpha derives from *ulfr* 'wolf' and O. E. *hege* 'hedge, enclosure'; Ekwall suggests that wolves may have been trapped there. As the Harringtons were a prominent knightly family of that romantic and beautiful district, it is logical that one of them should have become the folk hero of the story of the slaying of the Last Wolf, a tale which could well be founded on fact. Not all the place names in Cumbria which embody the world *wulf* however are derived from that animal. Some are a corruption of Ulf, a personal name, as in Ullswater (Ulf's water), Uldale (Ulf's dale) and so on. The actual date when wolves were finally exterminated in our district is not recorded although the slaying of the Last Wolf in Scotland by Sir Ewan Cameron of Lochiel has been placed in the year 1680.

Other traditional wolf stories include one of a Lady of Egremont who, while hunting with her lord, was separated from him, attacked by a wolf and torn to pieces. Her heart-broken husband, on finding her remains, cried out, 'Wo to this Bank', so that the name Wotobank has clung there ever since. Absurd though this derivation appears, the tradition itself may be based on an actual tragedy.

A similar story is told about the lady of Ulpha Old Hall in Dunnerdale who, pursued by a wolf in the gill near her home, leapt into a pool in the river and drowned. The pool is still known as Lady's Dub.

The Last Wild Boar slain in Southern Cumbria is claimed for the Kentmere Valley. There in the Hall lived the Gilpins, who are said to have received the manor by grant of King John, after one of them killed the monster which had been terrifying the inhabitants and preying on the flocks of the surrounding dales. Machel recorded the tradition in 1691-2. It is also claimed, however, that the Last Boar of Cumbria was slain on Wild Boar Fell by Sir Richard Musgrave of Hartley Castle (fl. 1409) near Kirkby Stephen. A farmhouse stands on the site but fragments of the rose red ruins of the castle can still be seen there. When Sir Richard's grave was opened in 1847, a wild boar tusk was found on his breast, which adds authenticity to the tradition.

The two immortal fish in Bowscale Tarn on the Skiddaw massif must not be forgotten. It was in this district that the Shepherd Lord Clifford was brought up in ignorance of his birth after his mother, Lady Clifford had married Lancelot Threlkeld of Yanwath and Threlkeld. During the Wars of the Roses and after Richard III — who owned Penrith Castle — came to the throne, the Lancastrian heir to the Clifford heritage would have been put to death, if found, by the Yorkists. The Shepherd Lord, devoted to nature and the study of the stars is described by Wordsworth as roaming the fells and lying in high summer by Bowscale Tarn in the fold of Blencathra where:

> Both the undying fish that swim
> In Bowscale Tarn did wait on him;
> The pair were servants of his eye
> In their immortality:
> They roved about in open sight
> To and fro for his delight.

The ballad of the *Nut-Brown Maid* in Percy's *Reliques* is thought by some to describe the Shepherd Lord's wooing of Ann, daughter of John St John of Bletsoe, who became his first wife.

A certain amount of folklore has grown up around birds. In Cumbria, as elsewhere, magpies are still regarded as augurs according to the number of those seen. As a child I was told:

> One is for sorrow, but two for mirth,
> Three's for a wedding, four for a death,
> Five for heaven, six for hell,
> But seven's the divil's oan sel'.

There was an alternative version taught to me as a child by a young, local maid:

> One's for sorrow, two's for joy,
> Three's for a letter and four for a boy.

I must admit that I still dislike seeing magpies and, as their number is increasing in Cumbria, the possibility of six or seven appearing at any one time becomes more likely!

Crows also are regarded as birds of ill omen but are useful as weather prophets:

> If crows be on the fallow,
> You'll be dry tomorrow,
> If crows be on the leas,
> You'll be wet to your knees.

A cock crowing near the door meant a stranger would soon arrive. 'Cockcrow' synonymous with 'sunrise' resulted in pagan times with the 'bird of dawning', being dedicated to Apollo. In the Christian period, one of the early Popes, perhaps to proclaim the ascendency of Christianity and also to assert that of the Church in the world, decreed that every church should be surmounted by a cock. One is depicted in the Bayeux Tapestry on a gable of Westminster Abbey. More recently the bird has been made to function as a weathercock, and since weather is fickle, some regard the vane as reminder and warning against St Peter's sin of betrayal. A Cumberland proverb strikes a lighter note:

A cock's aye crouse on its ain midden
(A cock's always bumptious on its own manure heap.)

Another weather forecast comes from Bampton:

A cock who goes crowing to bed,
Is sure to rise with a watery head.

A bird story somewhat resented by Borrowdale folk concerns the cuckoo. The remoteness of their dale and its narrow entrance inspired some of the natives to build a wall to keep the 'gowk' from migrating and so retain eternal spring. Of course the plan failed, but as the bird skimmed over the barrier, one of the disappointed dalesmen shouted, 'By gow! If we'd nobbut laid another line o' stanes atop, we'd a copped 'im!' This fictitious episode has resulted in the word 'gowk' becoming synonymous with 'fool'. Mr E. J. Field has found that many sites bearing the name 'Cuckoo Pen' or one similar, and associated with the 'pent cuckoo' story, are also linked with ancient earthworks. He therefore deduces that the ridicule directed against particular inhabitants of a district may stem from ancient enmities. Borrowdale certainly has its Iron Age Fort on Castle Crag and the place name springs from O. N. *borgar dalr,* 'valley of the *borg* or fortress' or from *borgar a,* 'river of the fort'. But I cannot trace any place or field name in the dale which contains the word 'cuckoo' or the dialect 'gowk'. Clarke in 1789 refers to the story as 'an old commonplace joke'.

Calendar
Lore

A CONSIDERABLE number of calendar customs are still spontaneously performed in Cumbria, though many — such as May Day celebrations, some of the ceremonies, and the occasional performance of Pace-Egging plays — are modern revivals of rites which were once a vital part of the traditional life of the community.

First Footing, on New Year's Day, is one of the customs still alive in the district when a dark man must be the first to cross the threshold of the house after midnight, otherwise if a fair man, child or women were to be the First Footer, ill luck would follow for the year. Right up to New Year 1971, I treasured each year the bread, coal and a penny which our dark First Footer, Bob Berry of Heathwaite, had been presenting annually for 20 years on being the first to enter our home on New Year's morning.

In 1900, a Caldbeck girl informed Mrs Hodgson of Newby Grange, that her grandmother would not allow water to be carried out of the house on New Year's Day. Water still had to be carried from wells at that time. Even today, in many places, nothing is allowed to go out of the house on New Year's Day until something has first been brought in, these customs point to the period when water and food were in short supply at times. In consequence the rule, 'Waste not, want not', which I well remember was a favourite maxim of my grandmother, was rigidly obeyed. Customs on New Year's Day tended to impose a pattern which was to be followed on all succeeding days of the year and the gifts of money – one penny – fuel – a piece of coal or wood – and food, a crust of bread presented by the First Footer were symbols, or perhaps luck auguries, to ensure that the inmates of the house would lack none of those necessities during the next twelve months.

Candlemas Day (2 February) is celebrated in the Roman Catholic Church by a candle procession followed by the consecration of all the candles to be used in services during the year. In pagan Rome candles were burned to the goddess Februa, mother of Mars, to drive off evil spirits, so that here is another example of the substitution by the early Church for a pagan festival.

The day was also regarded in Cumbria, as elsewhere, as foretelling the weather which would follow it. Mr J. C. Robinson of Staveley, Kendal has recorded some weather prophecies in dialect connected with Candlemas Day:

> If Cannelmas Day be cloody an' black,
> 'Twill carry away aw t'winter on it back;
> But if t'sun shine afoare it's neun [noon]
> Winter, depend on't isn't hawf deun [done].

Also:

> If Cannelmas Day be fine an' clear
> We'll hev twea winters i' ya 'eer.
> If Cannelmas Day be sunny an' warm,
> Ye may mend yer auld mittens an' luk fer a strom.

As the day was dedicated to the Purification of the Blessed Virgin Mary, an ancient Latin couplet repeats the weather prophecies:

> *Si Sol splendescat Maria Purificante*
> *Major erit glacies post festum quam fuit ante.*

> If before the Purification the sky with Sun is lit,
> More ice will follow after than came before it.

Mr Robinson gives an English version, stating, 'the source escapes me'. Recalling however, W.G. Collingwood's testimony to the high standard of scholarship often found among the countryfolk of the dales, when from Elizabethan times to the present day it was said in Bampton that farmers drove the plough in Latin; also that at Ulpha, college lads asking for their bill to be written in Latin were given one in Greek, it seems likely that the Latin weather couplet was known among dalesmen in the north west, at least before the Reformation – and in the original!

Mrs Hodgson in 1900 recorded a Candlemas saying from Dalton: 'If Candlemas be dull, shepherds will dance, if sunny they will mend their mittens', while Mrs Little of Patterdale in 1961 states:

> By Candlemas Day all geese should lay,
> And all good hogs do without hay.

The St Valentine's Day custom of sending an anonymous romantic greeting to a desired or accepted sweetheart is said to go back to the February Feast of the Lupercalia of pagan Rome. The names of favourite courtesans, written on tablets and placed in a box, were drawn by the gallants of the period who each accepted the name on his card as indicating the partner alloted to him by Fortune for the duration of the festivities. The Church later replaced the Lupercalia by a Christian festival, which was celebrated on St Valentine's day 14 February, and became associated with the sending of anonymous romantic greetings. An excellent account of local Valentines is given in *Cumbria,* where a charming card of 1878, sent to Anne Stables of Howtown near Pooley Bridge, is described. The original Valentine can be seen in Penrith Library museum.

Shrove Tuesday or Fasten Eve, the day before the opening of Lent, is still known as Pancake Tuesday and pancakes are made in the majority of Cumbrian households on that day. The custom of 'barring-out' the schoolmaster from his school was, up to the last decade of the eighteenth century, traditionally observed throughout

England on Shrove Tuesday. Indeed the Opies reported that it was still kept up at Tideswell, Derbyshire at least until 1938. In some places, barring-out took place at Christmas but W. Hutchinson in 1794 describes how 'until the last 20 or 30 years' it was customary at Bromfield on Shrove Tuesday, for boys to bar out the master from the school for three days. If he gained an entrance, school was resumed, otherwise the boys imposed terms regarding hours of study and play. Then a feast, a football match and a cockfight followed. The match was waged from the churchyard and the ball had to be deposited in the captain's house. The winners of the cockfight wore small silver bells on their hats for three successive Sundays.

At Patterdale, when the Rev. J. Hale was Rector (1892-8), barring-out had been transferred to Yak Bob Day (Royal Oak Day, 29 May). On one occasion the boys had successfully barred out both a schoolmaster and clergyman, much to the latter's annoyance and he brought a reluctant local carpenter to open the locked doors.

Shrove Tuesday at Scarborough marked the opening of the skipping, top and shuttlecock season. All three games began again around that time in Kirkby Lonsdale and Kendal, two places I knew intimately as a child. 'Booling' hoops came a little later, as, I think, did marbles, which were brought out around May Day.

The first of April and the first of May were reserved for making 'April Fools' − we called them April Noddies and May Geslings though, by a rule strictly followed, all tricks had to end by noon. Great was the delight in our household when anyone forgot the date, having been told to answer the door when no bell had rung, or shrieking with horror when warned of an imaginary spider crawling on his or her clothes, there were derisive shouts of 'April Noddy' or 'May Gesling'.

Religious festivals naturally played an important part in preserving ancient customs which, as we have seen, often had pagan antecedents. Easter and Christmas are perhaps the most outstanding dates in the Christian calendar which are associated with many traditional rites. One old rhyme taught to me about 1909 by May Howson of Hutton Roof refers to dates which precede and include the Easter festival:

Tid, Mid and Miseray
Carlin', Palm and Pace-egg day.

Tid appears to be a corruption of *Te Deum, Mid* doubtless refers to Mid-Lent Sunday, *Miseray* to the opening of the 51st Psalm *'miserere mei,* while *Carlin'* was Passion Sunday, the second before Easter Sunday when carlings, or dried peas, were softened overnight in boiling water, and eaten after being boiled with butter and seasoning the next day. Possibly Carlin' Sunday was a substitution for the Roman festival of Lemuria *(lemures* – spirits of the dead) during May, when beans were thrown on to the altar fires of the *lares* or household gods to pacify the ghosts of the dead. Lent is the period of mourning when church altars are draped in black. Mid-Lent Sunday was also known as Mothering Sunday. It was the fourth in Lent and during the Middle Ages was the day on which daughter churches and chapels sent congregations to attend the Mother Church for processions, services and alms-giving. At least three centuries ago the custom had developed in some places of letting apprentices and servants return home on Mid-Lent Sunday. It probably originated from the efforts made by the Mother church to gather together all who owed her allegiance. The Opies state that a Simnel cake was the traditional fare for Mothering Sunday, but in Westmorland the Simnel cake is still made and widely sold at Easter along with Hot Cross Buns. This fruit cake has a marzipan top edged with marzipan balls and often has a tiny nest containing coloured sugar eggs in the centre. Perhaps once the round balls were egg-shaped. The rhyme:

> Hot Cross Buns, Hot Cross Buns,
> One a penny, two a penny, Hot Cross Buns,
> If you can't give them to your daughters
> Give them to your sons.
> If you haven't got a penny, a half penny will do,
> If you haven't got a half penny, God Bless You.

is still well known, at least around Kendal and Kirkby Lonsdale.

Palm Sunday, which opens Holy Week, commemorates Christ's triumphal entry into Jerusalem. It is still customary in Cumbria and elsewhere to decorate houses and churches with pussy willow or 'palm', and with daffodils at this time. Pace Egg Day, in most places, in celebrated on Easter Monday, but in Lancashire on Good Friday. After Palm Sunday, Maundy Thursday before Good Friday had its own customs which were kept up on a small scale in Kendal and district until before the Second World War. On that day, local boys blacked their faces and hands, and paraded the streets, dragging old tins and buckets on ropes and chanting,

> Trot, 'errin', trot 'orn,
> Tis Good Friday tomorn.

They called at houses to collect pennies and pace eggs. The rhyme seems to refer to the end of Lent when herring which had been a staple food was being drummed out. The late Professor Edward Wilson of Kendal has recorded being accosted by some of these Jolly Boys, as they were called, on Good Friday 1936. It was at this same time that a small band called at my home in Kendal and were given money Professor Wilson asked them to repeat their song but they gave him the words of a popular song from the '20s:

> I haven't had an egg since Easter
> And now its half past three
> So chick, chick, chick, chick chicken,
> Lay a little egg for me.

Good Friday is observed as a day of mourning for the Passion and Death of Our Lord. The traditional fare for the day was Fig Sue, wheaten bread and figs boiled in ale, while Hot Cross buns were toasted for tea. Possibly the Fig Sue was made in reference to Christ's cursing of the barren fig tree.

Easter Sunday is to Christians a day of rejoicing for Christ's resurrection and was in the Middle Ages celebrated by a very beautiful and dramatic service in the churches. Up to the Second World War it was customary even for the poor and less prosperous to attend church in new clothes, symbolic of the ending of Lent and resurgence of life. J. O'Connor has described this aspect of traditional life at Easter in his *Memories of Auld Kendal*. But Easter Monday was the great day in Westmorland and Cumberland when, carrying their baskets of dyed and decorated 'pace' eggs (from *pasche*, Easter), boys and girls set out with their parents for the traditional rolling ground, where eggs were 'booled' against each other by two contestants, the winning egg being that least damaged.

In Kendal, Castle Hill was always the rendezvous on Easter Monday, in Kirkby Lonsdale it was Hollow Basin along the Church Brow; in Penrith, the Castle Moat; at Edenhall, Honey Pot Farm above the Giant's Caves. Each town and village had its traditional pace-egg rolling site and photographs taken before World War I show hundreds of children gathered there on Easter Monday. Jack O'Connor describes the singing game of Gandy Needles as performed when he was going on Castle Hill, Kendal, at Easter. A long line of lads and lasses faced each other, their hands joined and held high to form an arch. They sang:

> Grandy Needles, Grandy Needles, set, bump, set!
> Through the long lobby we go, we go,
> To see the bluebells, gee o', gee o',
> Open the gates so wide, so wide,
> And let King George, come through with his bride.

Meanwhile the top couple, bending low, went together 'through the long lobby', and joined both hands again at the foot of the column to complete the arch. The next couple at the top followed suit, until all had gone 'through the lobby'.

Besides 'rolling' pace eggs, another local game at Easter was 'dumping' eggs. This is played annually at the Black-a-Moor Hotel, Wigton, Cumberland. It was reported in the *Cumberland News* of 25 April 1957. Hard-boiled eggs, marked with their owner's number or initials, were placed in a large dish or strainer and gently shaken up. Cracked eggs were removed from time to time until, at last, one which had remained unbroken or only slightly cracked proved the winner. This particular game is recorded in Venetia Newall's *An Egg at Easter*, which Dr Robert Wildhaber calls 'this exciting and learned book'. It also contains not only beautiful coloured illustrations of decorated eggs but a comprehensive account of world-wide egg lore, traditions and symbolism, incuding that of our own district. The Wordsworth family pace eggs are mentioned and illustrated. These were decorated by the gardener, Robert Dixon when the family was at Rydal Mount. His photograph, along with eleven of the eggs which he had coloured, can be seen at the Dove Cottage Museum, Grasmere. Two other nine-teenth-century eggs of the Foster family of Allonby and Carlisle, decorated by a seaman relative, are included among the numerous colour photographs in this charming book.

During Easter, at Workington, the traditional game of football is still played. This is a quite different type of game from modern Association or Rugby, and resembles that played in the Orkneys as well as in the Scottish Border country and elsewhere. There is usually no limit to the number of players and, although there are goals of a sort these may be anything from 100 yards to several miles apart. The object of the game is for one of the opposing sides to succeed in carrying the ball back to their home base. At Workington one goal is the wall of Workington Hall, the other is a capstan at the harbour; the team known as the 'Downies' is drawn mainly from sailors, dock-side workers, the 'Uppies' are miners and steel workers.

The game opens with the ball being thrown up at a traditional spot by someone chosen as outstanding at that time. Since it has only been recorded since 1779, though played long before that time, it is difficult to decide on its origins. Some think it may have developed from some pagan rite performed in sun worship. However, it has many features in common with the original mass tournaments of the Middle Ages, and as such may be an imitation at a lower social level of those contests performed by knights and squires. Tournaments originally, as Old English football later, were waged by large bodies of men over a wide course. Knights and squires were mounted, whereas foot-ballers contended with their adversaries on foot, of course. Both contests assumed the character of warfare. Indeed in the sixteenth century football was played so fiercely that many of the contestants were seriously injured and as a result the game was forbidden by many authorities. Among the squires of the Middle Ages, also, their display of valour outran discretion and their participation in tournaments was forbidden. It has been suggested that football originated with the Normans and became popular throughout Normandy, Brittany, Ireland, Wales, Scotland and England, just as tournaments and later jousting spread throughout the countries of Europe. .

The Pace Egging or Jolly Boys play used also to be performed at Easter, on a succession of nights, by the young men of country districts who visited the farms in turn and performed it 'in front of the fire'. They were entertained to refreshments, as often as not a 'reet do' in the form of a substantial supper. There is not the space here to discuss the origins and symbolism of the play which was essentially a domestic drama performed in the homes of country folk by country folk. It is no longer performed except as a revival. Jonty Wilson, the well-known blacksmith of Kirkby Lonsdale who is now 84 (in 1975), acted parts in the play as a boy when living in the neighbouring hamlet of Biggins – as did Mr Clarke of Hollins Farm, near Kendal, who told J.H. Palmer in 1936 that 'he had taken part in many an Easter "Jolly boying" before the fire, which started with the entrance of the Fool, shouting:

> Stir up the fire and strike a light
> And see this noble act tonight.

The characters were usually Lord Nelson, Jolly Jack Tar, Toss Pot, Auld Molly Masket, St George, the Turkish Knight and Dr Jacky Brown. St George and the Turk fight, the latter is killed but restored to life by the Doctor, who asks the 'dead' man to open his thrippelty-thropelty and drink his nipelty-nopelty. The play ends with an appeal for money:

> So ladies and gentlemen who sit by the fire,
> Put your hands in your pockets and show your desire,
> Put your hands in your pockets and pull out your purse,
> And give us a trifle, you'll not be much worse.

In addition to Hot Cross Buns and Simnel cake, Easter Ledge or Sedge Pudding was also eaten at Easter. It is made from leaves of the red-shanked bistorts or Easter Sedge. Mrs Scott of Wigton Cumberland says that it was called Easter May Giant pudding and that her mother, born about 1870 near Caldbeck, Carrock Fell, had an old family recipe for the pudding as made by her great-great-grandmother. The bistort was called by country folk 'Ooster-munath-jonnums'. Mrs Scott referred to Ooster-munath as the very old name for April – 'Saxon I believe it is', she added. The ingredients for Easter Ledge Pudding in a collection of Cumbrian traditional-recipes are given as: equal quantities (about 1 lb.) of young bistorts and young nettles, a large onion, a tea-cup of barley, $\frac{1}{2}$ teaspoon salt. Chop greens and onion and sprinkle washed barley among them, add salt. Boil in a muslin bag for about 2 hours. Before serving beat mixture in a dish with one egg and butter and flavour with salt and pepper. Some people add a cup of oatmeal. The final mixture is recommended to be fried and eaten with bacon and eggs. The late Miss Carruthers of Heathwaite, Windermere made the pudding each spring in the 50's and used to cut the bistort from a bed on the Lane Head estate which then belonged to my husband's family.

In many parts of Europe water was believed between 11 and 12 on Easter night to have special powers bestowed on it. In Cumberland, John Shepherd of Gosforth Hall used to say that, at certain feasts, wine would be poured into the stream there which the villagers would look for and drink. This information Miss Senhouse collected in 1884. Unfortunately her informant did not specify on which feast the miracle occurred. The well at Bothel was supposed to run blood on the day of King Charles, the Martyr. In Cumberland, Westmorland and Yorkshire it was customary until into this century for country folk to drink water with sugar at their local Holy Wells on the patron saint's day. At Edenhall Miss Graham informed me that during her childhood in the 1920s Spanish water was always drunk on the third Sunday in May and was always referred to as 'Shaking Bottle Sunday'. Concerning this Brand writes:

> In the north of England it is the custom from time immemorial for lads and lasses from adjoining villages to meet at springs or rivers on certain Sundays in May to drink sugar and water . . . At the Giant's Cave near Edenhall a vast concourse of both sexes met for the purpose on the third Sunday in May.

The Rev. C.E. Golland draws attention to the place names of localities around Edenhall: Honey Pot Farm is but a stone's throw from the Giant's Caves of Isis Parlis. He suggests that *Isis* may be a corruption of the Celtic *Aesidhe* (Eeshea) or 'fairies' and that *Parlis* may be the Scottish *parrlie*, 'a small barrel', in popular speech, therefore, the Jars of the Fairies. Now the Musgraves of Edenhall acquired a Fairy Vessel or Jar which it has been suggested may have been used in the caves at some time for a pagan rite to the ancestors. This is treated more fully in the passage dealing with the Luck of

Edenhall. Honey Cakes were also eaten at pagan funerals, and arval bread and the soul cake are suggested as the modern equivalent of these. St Ninian's well, now practically forgotten, was near the caves on the banks of the Eamont, and the water-drinking ceremony on Shaking Bottle Sunday was perhaps all that remained in Protestant times of an originally pagan-turned-Christian rite performed at the sacred well. This idea is reinforced by the testimony of the Rev. E. A. Askew, who recorded in 1903 that around 1878 on the first Sunday in May the children of Greystoke went in a kind of procession to Tolly Well or Keld (dialect – t'oly well). They carried bottles in which were lumps of liquorice. After filling the bottles with well water, they were shaken until frothy and the liquid was drunk. The oldest inhabitants remembered the custom in 1903, but not its origin. I myself remember 'Spanish Water' being made in bottles in Kirkby Lonsdale as late as 1909, but tap water was used. It was a spring custom performed on no definite date for no particular reason except that – like various Spring games – it had always been done. In Cumberland 'Shaking Bottle Sundays' are still remembered as being formerly held in May but different places had a different Sunday for their performance, that at Eden Lacy Caves, near Great Salkeld, was held before the First World War on the first of May when 'The first of May is Shaking Bottle Day' was sung by those gathered there, for sports and drinking the special water, by one of the loveliest stretches of the Eden. The caves were constructed by Colonel Lacy in recent times.

In some places May Day festivals have been revived. At Melmerby the day has been celebrated in recent times since 1955. The eldest schoolgirl in the village becomes the May Queen, rides in state round the village green and is crowned on a dais erected there. A retinue of schoolchildren attends her, a royal proclamation is read and there is dancing round the Maypole. A wooden Maypole was erected on the Green at Wetheral in 1814 but was removed some 30 years later. A stone cross given by Mr Howard replaced the original Maypole. This was re-erected on its two-step platform but was removed from the centre of the Green and placed to one side so as not to interfere with the children's games. Most places had a Maypole and celebrated May Day with dances, feasting and games. Temple Sowerby had an old May Day competition, the winner being rewarded with a grindstone. The second prize was a whetstone and the third an inferior whetstone. The candidates aim was to tell the most wildly improbable story. Edmund Bogg in 1898 related that the Bishop of Carlisle, who was passing while the competition was in progress, declared he had never lied in his life, whereupon the Judge immediately awarded the whetstone to him.

Wrestling and racing usually ended the May Day festivities, and probably some sort of feast wound up the proceedings. It is significant that many of the Easter and May Day games and sports were held in ancient ring embankments, at Kirkby in Ireleth the Broomsgill ring, at Eamont near Penrith in King Arthur's Round Table. Others are listed in the *Place-Names of Cumberland.*

Royal Oak Day, Oak Bob Day or Yak Bob Day, is 29 May, the birthday of Charles II, commemorated by the wearing of a sprig of oak in memory of the tree in which the king hid and escaped capture after his defeat at the Battle of Worcester (3 September 1651). In 1816 branches of oak were used in profusion at Kendal when the *Westmorland Gazette* reported 'Kendal people made sad work with oak trees to decorate their doors on Royal Oak Day.' In 1883 the custom of 'barring-out' took place at Windermere School on Yak Bob Day and Mr J. D. Burrow of Crosthwaite recorded in 1940 that as a boy he had joined in barring out the master at Heversham Grammar School. The classroom floor was strewn with oak leaves and branches but, after ordering the boys to clear up the mess, the master granted them a holiday.

In 1888 carters were still decorating their horses and wagons with oak branches and the flag was flown on Kendal Town Hall to commemorate the day in 1900. As late as 1937 many boys at Windermere Grammar school still sported an oak sprig on the 29 May, and my daughter remembers that in Crook village certain boys who had forgotten their oak sprigs were offered a choice of 'muck or nettles' as a punishment. In Ulverston the Opies report that the day is named Bobby Ack Day; hair pulling is substituted for nettling while the song:

> Nob him once,
> Nob him twice,
> Nob him till he whistles thrice

is sung with actions to suit. Mrs E. Brocklebank of Millom, who

was born in Ambleside around 1910, remembers singing on the day
at school:

> If you don't give us a holiday,
> We'll all run away.
> Where will you run to?
> Down Stony Lane,
> Then old Mr Bently will come wi' his cane,
> An' quickly then he'll chase you all back again.

Mr Bently was then Head of the boys' school. About the same date
boys in Kirkby Lonsdale went about hitting with nettles any boys
who were not wearing sprigs of oak or Bob Apples.

St James' Day, 25 July, appears from the Rev. T. Machel's
journal of 1692 to have been a frequent date for Rushbearings in
Westmorland in the seventeenth century. He describes the occasion
at Burton in Kendale:

> On St James' Day they have a rushbearing. The young maids
> who perform the solemnity being entertained with music and
> such sort of Junkets as the country affords and there they dance
> about the Maypole, but none of their mirth is suffered to be
> enacted in the church or churchyard.

The custom arose through the necessity of having a dry and warm
covering for the damp earthen floors of churches and dwellings
before these were paved. The day of the saint to whom the church
was dedicated was at one time chosen for the ceremony until by an
Act of Convocation in 1530 all feasts of dedication were ordered to
be held on the same day.

The best-known Rushbearing in Cumbria, with the longest
continuous record, is that celebrated in St Oswald's Church,
Grasmere, though the ceremonies at Ambleside, Musgrave and
Warcop have also developed over the years a procession and ritual
of charm and dignity. The Grasmere Rushbearing is now held on
the Saturday nearest to St Oswald's Day (5 August). Today the
procession is led by the clergy, followed by St Oswald's banner. Six
girls in specially designed green and white tunics carry the linen
rush-sheet, hand-spun in 1891 by Mrs Wilson, and woven by hand

in Keswick. Choir boys and children carry the decorated 'bearings' – long poles with devices in flowers and foliage representing Moses in the Bulrushes, David's harp, crosses and circlets; but all contain some rushes, for everyone agrees that 'a bearing's nowt, wi'oot it hes rooshes'. A Maypole is generally carried, decorated with flowers and ribbons, for, as Machell pointed out, Maypole dancing and 'such sort of Junkets' followed the strewing of rushes in the seventeenth century. Before a local band became customary the procession was accompanied by a fiddler, who played the local Rushbearing March on the way to the church. About 1890 Mrs Fletcher wrote down the tune as Anthony Hall, who had succeeded old Jimmy Dawson as Rushbearing fiddler, played it to her on his violin. He was then 90 years old. During the nineteenth century a Hymn to St Oswald and another to be sung by the Rushbearers were specially written and music composed. After the service it has always been the custom to present to each Rushbearer a square of gingerbread, made according to the usual recipe. The Dixons have made this for over twenty years now and each section bears an impression of St. Oswald. The traditional Grasmere Gingerbread, made according to Sally Nelson's secret recipe now over 100 years old, is still sold at the shop in a corner of the churchyard and is more like a ginger and treacle shortbread or hard biscuit. Each child in the procession is given a 5p piece along with the gingerbread.

A picture if the Rushbearing at Grasmere was painted by Frank Bramley R. A. in 1905 and now hangs in Grasmere Hall, while a mural of the Ambleside procession by Gordon Ransome can be seen in the modern church of St Mary's in Ambleside where today's service is held. Formerly it took place in the old St Anne's off the steep road which leads to Kirkstone Pass.

Cumbrian fire customs were – with the exception of Guy Fawkes or Bonfire Night – abandoned during the present century. According to Dr Lyttelton, Bishop of Carlisle, the Midsummer Bonfires were continued in Cumberland down to the second half of the nineteenth century. But in 1692 Machel notes in his Journal that Midsummer Bonfires were no longer lit in Westmorland. Possibly the Civil War and the Puritan régime which followed brought an end to some old customs, or, since Guy Fawkes Night (5 November) has continued with unabated popularity into our own day throughout England, possibly all former bonfire celebrations, held at different times, may have been concentrated on that one date. It is, after all, only five nights after Hallowe'en when the Celtic *Samhain* was lit. It is interesting to recall that, up to the beginning of the nineteenth century, special cakes were made to be divided and eaten round the Beltane Fires in the Highlands, Western Isles, Perthshire and Wales. In many villages in Cumbria Bonfire Biscuits and Plot Toffee are still made to be eaten round the bonfire on 5 November. Ginger parkins and biscuits were given to spectators at Crook round the village bonfire when my daughter was a child about 1940. Perhaps ginger was regarded as a suitably 'hot' ingredient for fare on that night! The lines:

> Remember, remember, the Fifth of November,
> Gunpowder, treason and plot,

are well remembered though the complete version is not.

In the north of England fires were lit at Midsummer on what had been appointed by the Church as the Vigil of St John the Baptist. People gathered round the fires, lit in streets or squares, while young men leapt over the flames or engaged in sports; others ran with brands from the fire around the fields. In Dent on Guy Fawkes Night a young man ran with a lighted tar barrel up the cobbled street and back, then flung the blazing brand on the fire. This is probably a relic from times when the torch was carried round the fields at Midsummer or Midwinter. At Wetheral, in Cumberland, Midsummer Wakes were still held on the common until into the nineteenth century. From a huge bonfire, lit at night, lads kindled *tanlets* – long lengths of hemp soaked in pitch or tallow. With these blazing above their heads they ran through the village, a custom which probably originated like that at Brough, Normandy and other places, in the belief that evil agents would be expelled and fertility be bestowed upon all crops and herds which came within the vicinity of the fire. Pennant, in 1772, states:

> Till of late years the superstition of the bel-tin was kept up in these parts (around Keswick); and in this rural sacrifice it was customary for the performers to bring with them boughs of mountain ash. The berries of this mystic tree were the ambrosial food of the Celtic gods of Ireland.

Hallowe'en Fires were associated with festivals of the dead, especially with spirits of members of the family, believed to return to seek the comfort of their former homes on that night. As this was the period when in early times herds were brought into the shippons for winter, so folk held that the spirits of their kin had an equal right with animals to be welcomed under the ancestral roof. It was also believed that witches and fairies roamed about on Hallowe'en, and as the only certain way to destroy a witch was by burning, doubtless many suspected witches met their end on the Hallowe'en Fire.

Divination regarding marriage was especially practised on Hallowe'en around midnight. A true story concerning this was recorded by T. Carrick of Dalston and Wigton:

A servant girl in Hesket district was sent by her mistress at midnight into the barn which had doors opening to east and west to 'even the weights', i.e. to make a true balance on the weighing machine kept there. On her return the mistress asked, 'Did'st see out?' 'Nobbut t'maister', the girl replied, 'He come in at yeh door an' out at t'udder.' 'Be gud ta my bairns, then,' the mistress said.

A year later she died. The girl eventually married the master and proved a kind mother to her step-children.

Another method adopted by spinsters to divine their future husband on Hallowe'en was by making a 'dumb bannock', that is, preparing the dough without speaking, then going silent to bed after placing it on the baking griddle. The cook was then supposed to see in a dream her future husband turning the bannock.

Hallowe'en was also called in Cumbria *Hanchin Neet* from the game of *hanching* or snapping at apples hung on a string. The players hands were tied behind their backs.

Two other local fire ceremonies hold considerable interest. One, the Brough Holly festival, was held at Brough on Twelfth night, the Feast of Epiphany. This resembles a similar custom which used to be performed on the same night in Normandy where the builders of Brough Castle originated. T. W. Hewitson, writing in 1827-8, describes how the townsfolk supported by 'mine hosts' of the two leading inns in the town, procured a holly tree and tied to every branch a torch. These were lit at night and the blazing tree, carried through the town by Joseph Ling, a native of great strength, was

led by the band, accompanied by huzzaaing spectators, who also
carried torches. Marching up and down the streets they always
stopped before the cross on the town bridge where the holly was
greeted with cheers and the discharge of rockets and squibs. Finally
the almost burnt-out tree was fought for by two contending factions
each trying to carry the holly to the inn it supported. The successful
hostelry then provided a 'merry neet' paid for by the losing side.
Later and differing accounts are referred to in the Notes.

The Twelfth Night celebration in Normandy was performed by
men, women and children who ran wildly through the fields and
orchards beating their burning torches against tree trunks to destroy
lichen and drive away rodents. They believed that the fire not only
drove out all adverse agents but also brought fecundity to fruit trees
and crops, to flocks and herds. Possibly the original aim of the
Holly Tree festival on Twelfth Night was the same in Brough as in
Normandy and other parts of Europe held on the same night,
though W. H. Hewitson suggested that it commemorated the gifts
of the Magi symbolized at Epiphany by branches of holly and
evergreens being carried to church to decorate the altars. This,
however, contradicts a belief still widely current in Cumbria that it
is unlucky to leave Christmas decorations in place after Epiphany,
also that they must on no account be burned, but put outside.

The Need Fire must not be forgotten. Mrs Hodgson of Newby
Grange recorded from a Scaleby informant in 1901 that he knew of
cattle being driven through the fire in Cumberland during the cattle
plague of 1865-6. Mr Hodgson also had heard a rumour that the
Need Fire was then brought from Northumberland into
Cumberland. W. Wilson in 1887 records that the last time the
Need Fire was used in this neighbourhood (Keswick) was 1841.
Certain rules governed the lighting of the fire. All other
neighbouring fires had to be extinguished before the need fire was
kindled by the friction of wood on wood. Then all other fires had to
be rekindled from it after cattle and sometimes ailing human beings
were driven through it. Illness and disease were regarded until fairly
recently as the work of witches and the 'fire from heaven' was
supposed to offer protection against their spells.

The unquenched hearth fires in farms near Coniston are also
interesting. The Rev. T. Ellwood, Rector of Torver near Coniston,
writing in 1893, recalls how the hearth fire in Iceland in the

eld-house or fire-house in which the ancestral high-seat posts carried from their homeland were erected by the Norse settlers, was always raked out at night and the glowing embers covered with ashes or peat. The fire in consequence never went out. I remember that this was done on my grandmother's farm with the fire in the house-place (as the main living-dining room was always called) this fire was rekindled in the morning by putting dry sticks on the still glowing embers, then adding logs or peat. Probably the same method was followed in the kitchen, but that I do not personally remember. The Rector of Torver, however, knew one farm near Coniston where a fire had been kept continuously going for three generations. Another man claimed that he still had 'his grandfather's fire' and once when this accidentally went out, he took a shovelful of glowing embers from a neighbouring woodcutter whose fire had been lit originally from his. At Tullithwaite Hall, Underbarrow, near Kendal, the Women's Institute records that the fire never went out for 100 years, but the period when this happened is not stated.

In 1897 H. S. Cowper names these Coniston farms as the lonely moorland farmsteads of Parkamoore and Lawson Park on the fells east of Coniston. He quotes A. Craig Gibson who in 1864, had claimed that the farm fires were kept alight simply because of the difficulty of relighting them in days before lucifer matches had been introduced. Mr Cowper believed, however, that the custom was more likely to have originated in the ancient reverence for fire as an emblem of the fertilizing power of the sun, which was also regarded in another sense as an inimical power and I certainly believed as a child that sunlight actually extinguished fires.

Harvest Festivals are still very popular in Cumbria though today these are mostly celebrated by church services which are more than usually cheerful, being held in a beautifully decorated building amid a profusion of fruit and flowers brought as thanks offerings by church members. I remember the Harvest Festival sales on the Monday following, held in the church Sunday School room in the Congregational Church in Kirkby Lonsdale. These were very jolly affairs and greatly looked forward to annually in the first quarter of the present century.

T. Carrick of Wigton recorded in 1929 how in earlier times the 'luck sheaf' or the last one to be cut and bound was safely stored with an apple in it until Christmas morning. The apple was then given to the youngest daughter or maid and the sheaf to the best dairy cow. After supper at Harvest Home a dance was held, the master first dancing with the girl who had carried the luck sheaf off the field, the mistress with the head man or servant. A member of the Clifton Women's Institute records that Kern suppers were held after harvest each year; also, when the last sheaf of corn was bound someone would remember the traditional exclamation, 'That's the one we've been looking for all harvest!' A remark still to be heard on the harvest field.

Christmas is easily the most popular festival of the year in Cumbria as elsewhere in England, although it has now lost many of its traditional customs. How many housewives in Cumbria today still make their own Christmas cakes, puddings and mincemeat, while sweet pie is almost forgotten. My mother's recipe book – the paper brown now and fragile with age and use – contains not one, but many recipes for the same cake, pudding, wine or jam. The name of the donor is attached to some of these, witnessing to the interest of housewives in baking and cooking. It was not unknown, however, for a recipe jealously guarded by its owner, to be given to an importunate neighbour, lacking one of its important ingredients! The recipe for sweet pie, given in my mother's book dated 1894, was probably copied from *her* mother's recipes, just before she left home as a bride. Sweet pie had a rich suet crust and equally rich and very sweet ingredients. The crust was made from –

1lb. of flour with 8-12 oz. of finely grated suet rubbed in. Mix with water and roll to a 1 in. thickness.

Put into a pie dish:
½lb. currants
½lb. sultanas
½lb. shredded beef
¼lb. chopped suet
¼lb. grated mixed peel
½lb. chopped raisins
½lb. chopped apples
½lb. soft brown sugar
1 teaspoonful mixed spice or cinnamon.

Mix well, cover with the suet crust and bake in a moderate oven until the crust is golden. The pie must be served hot.

The rich ingredients of the pie are thought to symbolize the offerings of the Magi to the Christ Child. Hutchinson, around 1790, records this sweet pie being eaten for breakfast on Christmas morning in the parish of Whitbeck where it was called 'hack-pudding'. Sheep's heart being substituted for the beef in my family recipe. In that sequestered district the oxen were said to kneel at midnight on Christmas Eve and the bees to sing.

Two other traditional Cumbrian buns which appeared on the tea tables at Christmas – and at other times also – were cut and buttered, then eaten with rum butter or home made jam or jellies. These were Kendal wigs and double sweaters. The first were made from 1lb. of flour, 1½oz. lard, 1½oz. soft brown sugar, 1oz. yeast and a pinch of salt. Mix with milk or water. Add seeds or currants if liked. Double sweaters were tea cakes with two thick layers of sugared currants between.

Hanging the Christmas stocking on Christmas Eve is still popular among Cumbrian children. When I was a child little more was in it than an orange, an apple, a bag of nuts, one of home-made toffee, one small toy and perhaps a *Told to the Children* book. A Christmas Tree was essential, decked with coloured wax candles, with gaily wrapped parcels brought by Father Christmas beneath it. After supper all joined in songs and carols round the piano and there was never any lack of soloists. Cumbria is famed for its singing as witness the first Music Festival founded by Mary Wakefield of Kendal. Singing traditional songs was also an essential feature of Shepherds Meets, Merry Neets and other local festivities.

The traditional Christmas play was also performed in country districts until into this century. My mother remembered it being acted annually in the house-place of her home in Selside up to about 1890. This play was not unlike that performed by the Jolly Boys. It ended with John Funny asking for money:

> Here come I John Funny
> I'm the man who collects the money,
> Its money we want and money we'll have,
> If you don't give us money we'll sweep you all out.

Dancing was also very popular. At the last Christmas dance I attended at my old school – Queen Elizabeth's – in Kirkby

Lonsdale in 1917, then always held in the Institute in the New Road, the Lancers and Sir Roger de Coverley, Schottisches, and polkas — all vigorous dances — were very popular, but the traditional waltz, the valeta, barn dance and military two step were greatly enjoyed. The hall was always decorated with beautiful hot-house plants, palms and ferns provided by Dr Paget Tomlinson of the Biggins, then Chairman of the Governors. How nostalgic is the scent of geraniums and heliotrope bringing back memories of a quieter world before the First World War. Typical also of those more formal but courteous times were the small white dance programmes with pencils attached on which the initials of partners for each dance were written when they 'requested the pleasure' — what anxiety until the right initials had been inscribed for the 'supper' and last dance, always a waltz. I treasure some of those programmes still!

⟞ 8 ⟝

From Birth
to Burial

MANY OF THE customs and ceremonies concerning births and christenings are the same throughout England, and, up to at least the first decade of this century, it was usual in most towns and counties for those, who could not afford a local doctor or professional nurse to attend a birth, to call in a local midwife. Jack O'Connor has quoted from the *Westmorland Gazette* a first-hand tribute to the women of Fellside, Kendal, who ushered into their hard and difficult lives over two thirds of the children of that district. Mrs Jane Ann Willis, Mrs Ellen Stavert, and Mrs Tate (Mary White) were three local women who devoted themselves to perform this most helpful and necessary service. A woman in labour was referred to locally as being 'in the clouts'. Bishop Nicolson so refers to a Mrs Tatham – presumably one of his flock – in July 1712 as in this condition. The expression was still in use in Cumberland and Furness at least until 1903.

It was usual for the friends of middle-class women to be 'bidden' to attend births when confinement was imminent. These matrons were ceremonially summoned. A large china dish full of rum butter was usually prepared in readiness for 'the Day' and the new mother was the first recipient of what was regarded as a fine pick-me-up for women in her condition. The baby's head was washed with rum 'to strengthen it'. Rum butter is sold today in large quantities to tourists as being one of the local dishes and many Cumbrian families treasure their old china rum butter dishes as heirlooms. The christening feast was an important event. All relatives were naturally invited as well as friends. A Bampton member of the Women's Institute has recorded:

> At the christening, buttered sops were served, with rum butter. It was usual to present an egg and a pinch of salt to a new baby. (This is still done occasionally). Others give the child a silver coin.

Salt was regarded as imbued with power against fairies and ill-luck, as the many traditions concerning it testify.

Joseph Budworth has recorded in his Diary a recipe for buttered sops as made in 1792:

> The bread is cut in thin slices and placed in rows one above the other in a large kettle of 20 or 30 gallons. The butter and sugar are dissolved in a separate one, and then poured upon the bread, where it continues until it has boiled for some space and the bread is perfectly saturated with the mixture. It is then . . . served as a dessert.

A rhyme denoting a child's character according to the day on which it was born is still well known in Cumbria:

> Monday's child is fair of face,
> Tuesday's child is full of grace,
> Wednesday's child has far to go,
> Thursday's child is full of woe,
> Friday's child is loving and giving,
> Saturday's child works hard for its living,
> But the child that was born on the Sabbath day,
> Is blithe and bonny and good and gay.

That interest in the opposite sex develops early in life is shown by the many traditional children's games and various forms of divination concerning love and marriage which young people still engage in, in Cumbria. *Poor Jenny Sits a Weeping* for a lover, a singing game, is one, and *In and Out the Windows* shows the chief player standing to face his lover, before taking her off to London. The verse:

> Pippin, Pippin, Paradise,
> Tell me where my love lies,
> East, west, north or south,
> Carlisle or Cockermouth.

is sung while flinging an apple pip into the air. The direction in which the tip points when it has fallen is supposed to indicate the answer to the question.

By flinging the unbroken peel from an apple over the left shoulder with the right hand, it is hoped that the first letter of a lover's name will be formed. Several simple forms of divination are still used by children and young people:

> The counting of plum stones –
> 'This year, next year, sometime, never.'

> Pulling off daisy petals –
> 'He loves me, he loves me not.'

> Skipping to –
> 'Tinker, tailor, soldier, sailor,
> Rich man, poor man, beggarman, thief.'

The future husband is indicated by the word reached when the skipper fails to clear the rope.

The material of the wedding dress is shown by reciting while skipping – 'Silk, satin, muslin, rags'. The question 'How will I go to church?', is decided by chanting – 'Coach, carriage, wheelbarrow, cart'.

A few bodily symptoms are still thought to indicate the future, though not necessarily love and marriage. To shiver in Cumbria, as in most localities, is greeted with 'Someone is walking over my grave'. A rhyme about sneezing is still fairly well known –

> Sneeze on Monday, sneeze for danger,
> Sneeze on Tuesday, kiss a stranger,
> Sneeze on Wednesday, sneeze for a letter,
> Sneeze on Thursday for something better,
> Sneeze on Friday, sneeze for sorrow,
> Sneeze on Saturday, then comes tomorrow.

Love and betrothal were usually followed by marriage and, in the dales and country districts of Cumbria, this took the form of 'bidden weddings'. A 'bidder' was sent to 'lait' or 'round up' any who cared to come to the wedding and festivities which followed. Sometimes after the ceremony, guests raced on foot or horseback from the church to the reception for prizes. It was also customary for the bridegroom to fling handfuls of pennies amongst the crowd. The traditional 'sneckin' oop t' yeat' (fastening the gate) or tying a rope or ladder across the road to prevent the passage of bride and groom until a forfeit was paid died out in the early years of this century.

An interesting Cumbrian custom, no longer kept up, was followed when a girl was jilted. The lads of her village or neighbourhood then administered the doubtful consolation of rubbing her with pease straw. Girls performed the same service for a jilted youth. Pease straw appears to have been connected in some way with infidelity, as it was scattered on the road in front of the dwelling of anyone suspected of this particular transgression.

W. Henderson has quoted a verse from an old Cumbrian ballad about this custom:

> For Jock the new laird was new wedded,
> His old sweetheart Jenny linked na'e,
> While some were all titter'n and flytin',
> The lads rubbed her down wi pease strae.

One useful custom in the days before planning permission was introduced was that of 'clay daubin'. A young couple, having settled where to build their house – sometimes by squatting on wayside or common land – invited friends to help them and, in an incredibly

short time, by using crucks at each end joined by a roof tree, a clay
and wattle 'but and ben' was erected. While the men were digging
the clay, the women carried water to mix the clay with small stones
and chopped straw. The resulting mixture was then formed into
narrow sheets. These were rolled and carried to be unrolled between
thin layers of straw laid in courses three or four inches thick for the
walls. A thatched roof of straw or heather completed the building.
Robert Anderson has vividly described in verse the 'house warming'
which followed:

> We went ower to Deavie's Clay Daubin,
> And faith, a rare caper we had,
> Wi' eatin' and drinkin' and dancin'
> And rwoarin' and singin' leyke mad;
> Wi' crackin' and jwoakin' and braggin',
> And fratchin' and feightin' and aw'
> Sic glorious fun and divarshin'
> Was ne'er seen in castle or ha'.
> Sing hey for a snug clay biggin,
> And lasses that like a bit spwort,
> Wi' friends and plenty to gie 'em,
> We'll laff at King George and his cwort,
> The waws were aw finished er darkenin'
> Now greypes (forks), shouls (shovels) and barrows thrown by,
> Auld Deavie spak oop wid a hursle (shrug)
> 'Od rabbit it, lads, ye'll be dry!
> See, deame, if we've got a swope whusky,
> I's sworry t'rumm bottle's duin
> We'll starken our keytes, I'll uphod us,
> Come, Adams, rasp up a lal tune.

Adams was a well-known fiddler who, during the last century,
played jigs and strathspeys at the local fairs, merry neets,
kurn-suppers and clay daubins. In parts of the Lake District, where
stone and slate were plentiful, these materials were used in
preference to clay.

The more prosperous newly-wed bride and groom sometimes
decided to hold a bridewain in their own home. A general invitation
to this was advertized in the local paper or printed notices were sent

round. The *Cumberland Pacquet* of June 1803 published the following notice:

> Jonathan and Grace Musgrave purpose having a Public Bridal at Low Lorton Bridge End, near Cockermouth on Thursday the 16th. of June, when they will be glad to see their friends and all who may please to favour them with their company; for whose amusement there will be various races, for Prizes of different kinds; amongst others, a saddle and bridle; and a Silver tipped hunting horn for Hounds to run for. There will also be leaping, wrestling, etc. etc.
>
> Commodious rooms are also engaged for Dancing Parties in the evening.

It may be questioned how the expenses of such entertainments could be met, but it was the practice for the bride, towards the end of the bridewain, to sit enthroned with 'a pewter dribbler on her lap'. Then,

> The fwoak, leyke pez in a keale pot,
> Are yen through t'other mingling,
> An crowns an' hauf-crowns thick as hail,
> Are i' the dribbler jingling,
> Reet fast that day.

So generously did guests reward the bride that early in the last century at Keswick, £70 was donated at Henry Stoddart's bridewain, and at Holm Cultram £100 was contributed to another bride.

Another custom which aided newly-weds to get a start was that of 'corn-laiting'. It was seldom that a request from a young couple for a supply of corn or oat seed would be refused. Sometimes seed potatoes were asked for instead. Bishop Nicolson refers in March 1710 to Mrs Richardson of High House who was begging oats to sow. Perhaps she was a widow.

In spite of these various aids towards a good start the course of marriage did not always run smoothly as one ancient custom known in the north-west as 'Riding the Stang' demonstrated. Originally a way for the local community to express its disapproval of infidelity or cruelty in marriage, it was portrayed in a New Year's celebration at Appleby and described in the *Westmorland Gazette* of 1823. The local band headed a Fancy Dress procession through the town which included 'two antiquated figures of a man and woman, dressed in the fashion of other years, each mounted on a donkey'. Four years later the *Gazette* again reported New Year festivities at Appleby but added further information about 'Riding the Stang', a stang being the dialect word for a pole, which by this date appears to have been substituted for the donkeys. Formerly the characters whom it was the object to deride were represented by effigies dressed to resemble them closely. They were placed back to back on the donkey with their elbows tied together and the procession was accompanied by a jeering crowd beating kettles, drums and trays. In 1827 the Gazette condemned the custom as 'being used as a means for extorting money under circumstances which we think very disgraceful'.

It remains for John Lawson of Wetheral in a written description of about 1870-80, to throw further light on the matter. He also demonstrated how changed and decadent the custom had become. Indeed, by 1827 it had deteriorated into a mere means to extort money to be spent by the organisers on drink. Lawson in his notes describes how an armchair was fixed to a stang and decorated with ribbons. This was carried through the street preceded by a man with a flag and followed by the local band. Having seized and forced their first victim into the chair, they carried him some distance and extorted money from him. The amount was entered in a book and the man was offered a drink by the official bottle-and-glass carrier. The company then went off to capture another victim. This continued through the day and the proceeds were devoted to a 'Merry Neet', at the local pub, with drinking, singing dancing and story telling. These sessions sometimes continued for two nights and a day. The last Stanging in Wetheral was held in 1850 at the Fish Inn.

At Langwathby, near Edenhall, Riding the Stang was still imposed in 1896 on anyone found working during the Langwathby Rounds, at that time still a popular festival. Payment of a forfeit freed the victim from having to undergo the Ride. Even in 1930 there were old people in Kirkby Lonsdale who could remember the Stang being ridden.

We have seen how professional aid was not always called in at births, and this was equally so with regard to simple ailments. A. Pearson vouches for the truth of the use of extraordinary home treatments for various forms of illness as late as 1930 in Kirkby Lonsdale and the surrounding districts. A concoction of slugs potted in salt and eaten on bread was regarded as beneficial for anaemia; slugs being full of electricity, help to make new blood for the body! Bronchitis, it was claimed, would be cured if a piece of brown paper shaped like a heart were covered with goose grease and worn on the chest.

The Rev. H. H. Bulkley recorded in 1885 the instance of a boy in East Cumberland who was tortured by toothache. The local blacksmith prodded the decayed tooth with a rusty nail, then, after blindfolding the lad, led him to an oak tree and told him to hammer in the nail. That done, he restored the bandage he had removed, led him back to the smithy and made him swear he would not try to find the tree or tell anyone else about it. Then he assured the boy he would have toothache no more. We are not told whether the assurance was justified!

When death occurred in a Cumbrian household the custom of telling the bees was followed into this century. The hives were gently tapped and the bees were told who had died. To placate them further, crumbs from the funeral feast were given to them; unless these courtesies were observed it was feared the bees might fly away. My husband remembered this being done on a farm in Underbarrow near Kendal around 1916. The passing bell was rung in Kirkby Lonsdale and probably in other places as late as 1930, but this, in spite of its name, took place after death had occurred and the number of tolls proclaimed to neighbours that the man (if 5 tolls), woman (if 4) or child (if 3) had passed away. The number of tolls rung to indicate these particulars varied with each parish. Bells were originally believed to frighten off evil spirits and to help the soul on its journey.

Arrangements were then made for the funeral. The same women who helped as midwives acted as 'layers-out' when poorer families were bereaved. A 'bidder' was also sent round to invite people to funerals. Jackie Mallinson of Edenhall describes how he and his brother, as schoolboys, trudged on many occasions round the parish to outlying farms to bid these neighbours to a funeral. It was an affront to both dead and living to refuse. He also recalls that a small table with a white cloth was placed outside the door of the deceased on the day of the funeral. It held a vase or basin with sprigs of box or yew in it. Mourners took a sprig to drop on to the coffin after it had been lowered into the grave. Old people can remember arval bread or biscuits being given to those who attended a funeral. Some think the word *arval* means 'inheritance' while others that it derives from an ancient Scandinavian word for funerals. It is still the custom in Cumbria for the deceased's next of kin to invite relatives and all who have attended the funeral from a distance to join in a meal or refreshments, after the ceremony.

Up to the first decade of this century, if the deceased's family were not well-to-do, his relatives or close friends would carry the coffin to the church on their shoulders, though usually a great effort was made to hire a hearse and carriages. Jack O'Connor has described one of these earlier funerals in Kendal:

> The duties entailed in the office of Funeral Bidder were of a very highly diplomatic nature – who was or was not to be asked back for a cup of tea after the burial. The bidder took the rap if things went awry. The most likely men to be asked were those who, on many occasions, not only lifted the coffin on to the trestles outside the cottage door, but, having sung a hymn, took turns in carrying the coffin right through the streets to the cemetery on their shoulders, thus cutting, not only their shoulders, but the expense of those who shouldered the burden of meeting the funeral bill.

Funerals – even if there was a horse-drawn hearse and carriages for the chief mourners – went at a 'funeral pace' to allow the many who followed on foot to keep up with the cortége. All who met a funeral stood still as a sign of respect, and men doffed their hats, at least until the coffin and chief mourners had passed. This slow style of funeral caused a suspension of traffic and was impossible after motor transport became common.

In earlier days the coffin was carried from outlying farms strapped on to packhorses. During the period when many districts only had chapels, parishioners were compelled to be married and buried in the Mother Church of the district. This often lay at a considerable distance over wild mountain tracks. The roads over which bodies had to be carried for burial are still known as 'corpse ways'. The scattered inhabitants of Firbank and Killington living among the remote fells of Westmorland petitioned in 1595 for permission to have rights for Sacrament, Divine Service and Burial at Killington Chapel:

> As they have at present at the parish Church of Kirkby Lonsdale as none of them lives less than six and some of them ten miles from that church, and by reason of storm and floods and the like, their journeys to attend services, baptisms and burials are extremely perilous.

I myself remember my terror as a small child around 1909 being taken across the Lune by the ferry boat from Hall Beck Farm, Killington, when the river was in spate. Such journeys were fairly common within living memory, and it is pleasing to know that the Killington petition was granted.

One of the wildest of these corpse roads was that from Wasdale Head to Eskdale over Burnmoor. This is said to be haunted by a galloping horse carrying a coffin. The story is that a young man, the only son of his mother, had died and was taken by packhorse for burial on a misty winter's day. The horse took fright and bolted, and the mourners search – hampered by fog – was fruitless. On reaching home, the deceased's mother collapsed and died. During her funeral, near the same spot where her son's horse had bolted, her packhorse also got away, Again, the search was hindered, this time by snow. But though the mother's horse and coffin were not found, those of her son were. He was duly buried. The mother's body, however, was never recovered, and the ghostly steed haunting the moor is thought to be hers, still carrying her coffin.

—⊃9⊂—

Traditional
Life

IN REMOTE districts of Britain such as Lakeland, the coming of the railways did not alter the traditional way of life in many of its districts and dales as much as is sometimes claimed. Not until motor transport was developed, with consequent changes in agriculture following the introduction of the internal combustion engine, was the old style of Cumbrian life and manners seriously affected. Many small towns, like Kirkby Lonsdale and Ambleside, were at least two miles from a railway station, and no buses connected them at that time with larger centres, so that many like them, together with innumerable villages, hamlets and farms, remained, up to and beyond the First World War, comparatively isolated.

I can personally clearly recall as a child visiting the farms of two relatives — one near Kirkby Lonsdale, the other at Selside near Kendal, where a style of life now completely vanished was followed. In each, there was a cheese room: on shelves round the walls were stored 30-40 huge, as well as smaller, round cheeses, made on the farm. In the slate-floored down-house, where the main

139

domestic work of the farm was done, stood the cheese press and big polished churn. How delicious new whey and buttermilk tasted then! The cool dairy with its wide slate shelves held rows of brown and yellow earthenware crocks in which the new milk stood until cream set on the surface, to be skimmed off daily into tall brown jugs ready to be made into butter on churning day. Huge wooden dishes of newly gathered eggs stood there waiting to be taken each week to market; butter, freshly worked into round or oblong pounds and imprinted with a thistle or rose, acorns or perhaps a heart and leaf pattern, were all packed weekly into special wooden butter boxes and carried by trap into Kendal or Kirkby Lonsdale, to be sold in the Market Hall.

Outside the farm house was the corn shed with huge bins of grain or 'Indy' corn (maize) and Bibby's meal cake for the calves. How thrilling to bring down cows and calves from the upland paddock for milking the low cobweb-hung shippons — unhygienic perhaps, but when were we harmed from drinking milk warm from the cow? — to feed the calves from their row of buckets and whack the greedy ones which tried to steal 'poddish' from their neighbours; to rake, toss and make the hay and have 'drinking' brought out — tea in big blue enamelled billycans, with sandwiches, home-made cakes and pasty in big old-fashioned baskets covered and lined with linen napkins; and to help tie the sheaves with bands made from two thick strands of corn stalks twisted together. How often hands got pricked with thistles hidden in the corn! Then to ride with hay or corn into the barn and slide from the top of the 'hay-moo'. At last, to go in to a supper of buttered oatcake and new milk or a dish of barley boiled with milk and raisins. What bliss to be allowed to sit up late round the fire listening to country gossip. Then — a final joy, though slightly scaring — to go to bed in the flickering light of a candle instead of by gaslight, as at home, knowing one would wake in the morning to country sounds — the clang of buckets; calling the calves to feed with 'Coosh, coosh, coosh', just as sheep were called when being laited by 'How, how, how'; aunt's voice, 'Chuck, chuck, chuck' with the fall of corn and the cackling of hens. How infinitely more satisfying than the smells of petrol, the grinding of cars and crash of gears, and the square, unattraction of baled hay, bound by machine, instead of the nursery rhyme haycocks set up by hand.

Sheep farming has many traditional occupations connected with it. Herdwicks are the native breed of sheep, though the name referred originally to the pasture where the sheep were kept. The story that they are descendants of a flock from a ship wrecked on the Cumberland coast after the defeat of the Spanish Armada, or, in an alternative version, from a foundered Norse vessel, is not thought to be true. The breed is, however, well suited to the hard life of the fells. They can withstand severe weather and shortage of food, and are able to live on coarse grass and heather shoots. In addition they like to keep to their own 'heaf' — that area of the fell allocated to a particular farm and its flock, part of which belongs to the landlord. These 'stock sheep' are handed over with the farm on a change of tenancy at a traditional 'viewing'. Each farm also has a distinctive ear or 'lug' mark by which a farmer can identify his own animals. Sheep also often receive a 'smit' mark after shearing — an initial or other distinguishing mark is smeared in ruddle or some other dye on their coats.

The old Celtic numerals were used for counting sheep up to the last century. Number one was *yan* round Coniston and Borrowdale. This is still the commonly used dialect word for 'one'. *Un* was 'one' in Old Welsh and *un* and *unan* in Cornish and Breton, while five was *pimp* in Lakeland, *pimp* in Old Welsh and *pymp* and *pemp* in Cornish and Breton. Ten was *dick, dec, dek* in the respective dialects. It is thought that these numerals and the others in between were based on a system of counting in fives. There were slight local differences in the numerals as used in different dales.

Shepherd's Meets are still held in Cumbria for the purpose of allocating stray sheep to their owners. Hound trailing has replaced horse racing and wrestling as diversions at these gatherings, but a Merry Neet with a tatie pot supper, drinking, and the singing of traditional and other songs, still winds up proceedings.

Sheep farmers always need well-trained dogs to aid them in laiting their sheep to bring them down from the fells for shearing and dipping. Each collie or sheep dog has to be trained to obey his master's orders. Some farmers give directions by calls and whistles, others by signals with a stick or by a mixture of all three. It takes about two years for a dog to be fully trained. The more intelligent and skilful dogs are entered for Sheep Dog Trials held at Rydal, Troutbeck and other centres. These dogs are not only able to pen a single bunch of sheep very quickly, which — to them — is a comparatively simple operation, but they are also skilful 'shedders', that is, they are able to pen two sheep from say, a group of six, and divide the remaining four into couples and pen these into separate folds, while keeping those already penned from escaping into the open again. These operations depend on the partnership of dog and master, and it is a thrilling experience to attend a Sheep Dog Trial and witness the astonishing and complete rapport which exists between men and dogs, both often the descendants of generations of sheep tenders. Some dogs are also skilful 'markers' — with a special gift for finding sheep buried in the snow. On locating a buried animal, the dog begins to dig furiously and is quickly aided by the farmer. If the sheep is too weak to be moved, food can be brought to it until it regains its strength.

Another traditional skill which developed in the sheep-rearing dales of Cumbria and Yorkshire was that of hand knitting. This industry was recorded in the sixteenth century. In Elizabeth's reign the change from distaff to spinning wheel enabled a single spinner to provide enough yarn to keep four or five knitters constantly working. The so-called 'spinning galleries' found on some Lakeland farms as at Thorn House, Low Hartsop and Yew Tree Farm, Coniston were probably used for hanging cloth after finishing, for storing peat and farm implements. They also gave access to the upper floors. In Cumbrian farms and cottages all members of the family knitted, including the men, shepherds tending their sheep, wagoners driving their teams, women walking or driving pillion to market, and during or between household tasks. Children were taught to knit as soon as they could manipulate the needles. At Kendal, around 1770, the knitting of stockings with its attached skills, employed over 5,000 workers. These knitters worked at great speed. This was attained by the wearing of a belt round the waist, into which a knitting stick or sheath was tucked at the right hand side to support a needle. Examples of these sticks can be seen in Lakeland museums in a great variety of shapes, materials and decorations. Another aid to speed was the habitual rhythmic motion of arms and body called 'striking the loop', often performed to the accompaniment of a song. One of these was communicated to Mrs Hodgson of Newby Grange in 1900:

> Bulls at bay,
> Kings at fay,
> Over the hills and far away.

'The terrible knitters of Dent' were the most famed hand-knitters of the northern dales. This village near Sedbergh with its cobbled streets has retained much of its old-world character. Adam Sedgwick, its most famous son, has quoted an old song in his reminiscences of Dent:

> A clever lass in Dent
> Knaws how to sing and knit,
> Knaws how to carry the kit [milk pail]
> While she drives her kine to pasture.

Girls from the Lake District were sent to Dent to receive training from the stalwart knitters there. Betty Yewdale and her sister Sally went from Langdale to Dentdale for this purpose when only seven and five years old. Though kindly treated, they hated the coarse food and must have found the gruelling work very hard. Worst of all they were desperately homesick. Betty, when old, described in dialect their experience of knitting under very hard conditions. Sarah Hutchinson, Mrs Wordsworth's sister, wrote down her account:

> We went to a Skeul about a mile off — ther was a Maister an Mistress — they larnt us our lessons, yan a piece — an then we o' knit as hard as we cud drive, strivin, which cud knit t'hardest, yan against anudder — We hed our Darracks (day's work) set afore we come fra' heam in t'mornin'; an' if we deedn't git them dunn we warrant to gang to our dinners — They hed o' macks o' contrivances to larn us to knit swift — T'maister wad wind 3 or 4 clues togedder for 3 or 4 bairns to knit off — that at knittest slawest raffled tudder's yarn, and than she gat weel thumped .... Then we ust at sing a mack of a sang, whilk we were at git t'end on (which we had to get to the end of) at every needle, ca'in ower neames o' t'fwoak in t'deeal — but Sally an me wad niver ca' Dent fwoak — seea we ca'ed Langdon (Langdale) fwoak — T'sang was —

> Sally an' I, Sally an' I,
> For a good pudding pie,
> Taa hoaf wheat, an' tudder hoaf rye,
> Sally an' I for a good pudding pie.

We sang this altering t'neams at every needle; an' when we coom at end cried 'off' an' began again, an' sea we strave on, o' t'day through. Neet an' Day ther was nought but this knitting . . . .

At last, one snowy night the children – very scantily clad – ran away. They reached Sedbergh and spent a night in an inn. Next night they found shelter in a poor woman's house in Kendal but shared a room with an old dame who had fits! Not until 2 a.m. the next morning did they reach Langdale, footsore and hungry, little guessing that their story would be made immortal by Southey, the Poet Laureate.

Goods made in the dales, as well as raw wool, had of course to be transported to centres where they could be sold, and long trains of packhorses travelled along tracks and roads performing this service. A list of these trains which carried wool and goods from Kendal, Cockermouth, Penrith and other Cumbrian towns to London each week towards the end of the eighteenth century shows that 234 horses were making the journey regularly. Letters were also carried between trading towns and Roger North commented that these were delivered and answers carried back as certain as by post.

Wagons, carriages, regular passenger coaches and travellers on horseback, with maybe their wives riding pillion, were all to be met with on the roads, which were improved by the establishment of turnpike trusts after 1750. In consequence of all this, inns too were improved. Many of these ancient coaching inns still exist in the area and many retain some of their traditional features if not their old atmosphere. Christopher North has left a description of a typical Lakeland breakfast of around 1810:

> Mrs Bell of the Red Lion Inn, Grassmere, can give a breakfast with any woman in England. She bakes incomparable bread . . . . What butter! Before it a primrose must hide its unyellowed head. Then jam of the finest quality, gorse, rasp and strawberry . . . . Hens cackle that the eggs are fresh – and those shrimps were

scraping the sands last night in Whitehaven sea. What glorious bannocks of barley meal, crisp wheaten cakes too! Do not, our good sir, appropriate that cut of pickled salmon . . . . One might live a thousand years and yet never weary of such mutton ham . . . .

And so he continues extolling the 'virgin honey', cold pigeon pie, beef steak with potatoes. All this just for breakfast! Which leaves one marvelling what could then be left for other meals.

Many legends are told of these old inns. One amusing anecdote accounts for the changing of the name of *Barngates Inn* near Hawkshead to that of *The Drunken Duck*. A barrel of beer had burst in the inn yard and a duck, which had drunk deeply of the liquor, fell down senseless. The innkeeper, thinking it was dead, asked his wife to pluck it ready for cooking. She did so and put the bird on a slab in the dairy. The cold revived it, so that it waddled out into the yard quacking loudly. Whereupon — so it is said — the landlady, feeling sorry for the naked bird, quickly knitted it a jersey of Hawkshead wool to wear until its feathers grew again!

Two inn names recall the packhorse trains and the wool trade — *The Fleece* Inn and *The Woolpack*, in Kendal; others remind us of horse traffic — *The Horse and Farrier* at Threlkeld — while several *Travellers' Rests* hint at the many who in former days went from place to place on foot. Among these were the packmen and pedlars. I well remember an old blind pedlar who travelled the Kirkby Lonsdale district with his black pack and guide dog. His name was Parker and he sold tea to outlying farms, where he was often given a good meal. He died worth several thousand pounds. This was in the period just prior to the First World War. Mrs Brockebank of Millom also records that around 1930 a woman pedlar called 'Old Mary' carried tape, buttons, cotton and pins in a clean white bag to outlying farms. Visiting tailors and seamstresses also travelled the roads until around 1920. They visited families who regularly employed them, making up materials supplied by their employers. A Martha Chamley, in my grandmother's day, used to stay at her farm and others in the Selside district near Kendal, doing necessary sewing and dressmaking for the family. Mrs Proctor from Biggins, near Kirkby Lonsdale, performed the same service for families in that district. Although elderly, she regularly walked to and from her home to houses a mile or more away, sometimes in bad weather, returning each night on a hilly road after at least eight hours work.

Tailors in the earlier period were sometimes able to sing and recite, and in any case had collected all the news of the district, so their visits were greatly enjoyed, especially on lonely farms where they often stayed a week.

In 1958 Alfred Langstrath recorded the reminiscences of Mr J. W. Holt of Bassenthwaite concerning his early life as a journeyman tailor before the First World War. Such a tailor was then known as Tommy or Johnny Whipcat and his visits were called in Cumberland 'whipping the cat'. Sometimes a farmer employing Mr Holt and his uncle, to whom he was apprenticed at the age of 15, would arrange to collect them and their cumbersome sewing machine in his trap. But Mr Holt recalled:

My uncle and I set out for Millstone Moor about 9 or 10 miles away. We carried our tools, including a very heavy iron. The farmer, Mr Tom Atkinson, was sent to meet us with the horse and trap. I don't know whether he slept in or couldn't catch the horse, but we walked to Isel school, six miles from home, before we met him.

Journeymen tailors were paid half-a-crown a day, but received board and lodging in addition. They used 'goose irons' to press the suits. These were large and heavy, so huge fires had to be kept up to heat them. Here, perhaps mention should be made of the small traditional charcoal heater, used by housewives then for roasting sticks of charcoal in a red fire. The sticks, when glowing, were placed in the box-iron which was filled up with more charcoal and the top clamped down. The charcoal heaters were simply made from thick wire with a long handle attached to a spiral shaped cup in which the charcoal was placed for heating. I recently saw one of these objects labelled in a museum as an apple roaster. The custodian said that no one knew its real use.

Sheep affected not only industry and travel in Cumbria but at least one pastime, if hunting can be called a pastime in a district where it is vital to a great proportion of the inhabitants to keep down the number of foxes. Hunting is followed on foot, for the fox travels great distances when pursued, up the steep dales and over fells and crags, where it would be impossible to ride a horse. John Peel, a typical farmer huntsman of Cumberland, has become part of the folk and legendary lore of Lakeland and his reputation is now world wide. Perhaps this is mainly due to the popularity of the song 'D'ye Ken John Peel?' written by his friend John Woodcock Graves. The poem was composed one night in 1832 while the two friends were sitting in the snug parlour of the cottage, still to be seen in Midtown, Caldbeck. Above the doorway the letters and date TBB 1718 are inscribed. When he had finished writing, Graves pushed the words towards Peel and said, 'By gok, John, thou'll be sung when both of us is run to earth!' This prophecy has come true. Graves' version of the song describes Peel's coat as 'so grey' — not gay. The material was probably made in Graves' own mill at Caldbeck. Here 'hodden' or 'Skiddaw grey' was woven from the undyed wool of local sheep. Graves also recorded that Peel lived 'at Caldbeck' not 'at Troutbeck', once on a day. The house on the small estate at Ruthwaite was bequeathed to John's wife by her father and can still be seen, as can John's grave with its well sculptured head-stone in Caldbeck churchyard. As Peel's cortége passed the kennels, his faithful hounds set up a mournful howl, deeply moving to those who heard it. He died 13 November 1854 in his 79th year. Graves, who had emigrated to Tasmania, was 91 when he died there. He painted several pictures of John Peel. One shows him blowing his horn, with Ruthwaite and the Skiddaw range behind him and his hounds at his feet. This was sent to his friend T. McMechan of Wigton, and after many vicissitudes the portrait is back in Wigton, having been bought in 1966 at Sothebys by Maurice Redmayne.

The popularity of the song is largely due to its stirring tune. Originally set to the old folksong *Bonnie Annie,* the accompaniment and air was rearranged in 1868 by William Metcalfe, organist at Carlisle Cathedral, since when it has been sung and danced to round the world.

Cockfighting and wrestling became two of the most popular sports in Lakeland. Cockfighting was made illegal in 1835, but continued to be followed in secret. One good example of a cock pit is in the garden of Greenbank, Horncop Lane, Kendal, where a garage has now been built into it. Others can still be seen at Heversham, Orton and at Patterdale, as well as in Furness at

Oxenpark. There is a particularly good example south-west of Ulverston at Stainton.

In spite of, or perhaps because of, its brutal character, cocking used to be popular in schools. It was enthusiastically encouraged by the boys' fathers, who willingly gave the required cock pennies, which varied in value from 6d. to a 20s. piece in gold. The latter coin was contributed by Sir Daniel Fleming of Rydal when his son Henry was captain. The purpose of the cock pennies is not quite clear. Some think it went towards the payment for cocks provided by the schoolmaster to oppose the birds brought by his pupils. Clarke in 1787 suggests that the money went towards the master's salary.

The contests were supposed to encourage the fighting spirit of the boys through witnessing the courage displayed by most of the cocks. We have already mentioned that cockfights were held as part of the Shrovetide celebrations. This association of the game with the festival in schools goes back to at least Henry II's reign, as London records show.

Wrestling probably succeeded archery as one of the skills in which Cumbrian youth loved to excel. During medieval and Tudor times the yeomen of Cumberland and Westmorland, clad in traditional Kendal green, were famed for their prowess with the longbow. A special Cumberland and Westmorland style of wrestling developed in Cumbria. This continues to be seen at contests held at various local gatherings in the district. The origin of the sport is not known, but it may be significant that the earliest folklore concerning Hugh Hird, the Kentmere giant, makes him a champion archer when reported in 1692, but a century later he is famed in popular memory as a great wrestler who can overthrow London champions. There is no space here to give a full account of this traditional sport in Cumbria, but interesting details are provided in W. Rollinson's *Life and Tradition in the Lake District*.

Fairs, much more numerous up to the beginning of this century, were once very much part of the traditional life of the countryside. Appleby Fair, still attended by hundreds of gypsies in their traditional horse-drawn caravans, beautifully decorated and carved, is mainly concerned with the sale of horses. It is held in early June. Cockermouth still holds what was originally a Hiring Fair at Whitsuntide and Martinmas. These fairs originated in the passing of the Statute of Labourers in 1349 when all labourers were ordered to repair to the nearest market centre on certain dates to offer their labour for hire. F. W. Garnett has described a scene at a hiring fair held in the early years of the present century:

> Men and women stand in the market place on the appointed day, the former wearing some token in their coats and hats, a straw generally in former times but now commonly an artificial flower, as an indication that they were unhired. The farmers pass among them and, selecting a likely looking man or woman, the bargaining for wages commence (sic).

The bargain was completed by the farmer handing the servant a shilling, known as a *yearl* or *arl,* as a binding acknowledgment for a half year's service up to the next hiring day. A week's holiday followed in which the servants-to-be attended any local fairs or races, wrestling and cockfighting displays during the day, and ended by dancing and drinking at night.

Egremont Crab Fair has been held continuously — except during the two World Wars — since 1267 when Thomas de Multon, Lord of the Barony of Egremont (1247-1294), granted a charter to the town for an annual fair to be held on the nearest Saturday to 18 September. The title probably stems from the traditional free distribution of apples — originally crab apples — from the apple cart which is paraded through the main street on the morning of the fair. A Gurning Competition is a main attraction during the evening. Competitors for the World Gurning Championship peer through a horse collar — the braffin — and the winner is the one considered to have pulled the most grotesque face. Gordon Mattinson, a Cumbrian, was 'king of the ugly mugs' in 1974. Cumbrian children who are looking sulky are still bidden by their mothers to 'Stop gurning!'

Hours were long on the farms, wages were small, the accommodation given to farm servants was often of the poorest, and food of the simplest and, unless the servant had made sure beforehand that his farm was 'a good spot' for food, this might easily be insufficient. On the more prosperous farms, however, conditions were usually good. Many of those who began life as farm servants were farmers' sons who eventually secured farms of their own, and, until the coming of motor transport and powered machinery, together with the introduction of radio and television into their homes, traditional ideas, customs and techniques were followed which have now become, within living memory, things of the past.

Notes and Abbreviations

A.A.	*Archaeologia Aeliana*
Antiquity	Quarterly review of Archaeology
Cumbria	Monthly Magazine on Lake District Life
CW 1, CW 2	*Transactions of the Cumberland and Westmorland Antiquarian and Archaeological Society* – Old and New Series
C.W.(R.S.)	*Cumberland and Westmorland Antiquarian and Archaeological Society* (Record Series)
C.W.(T.S.)	*Cumberland and Westmorland Antiquarian and Archaeological Society* (Tract Series)
I.H.M.W.	*Inventory of the Historical Monuments of Westmorland*, Royal Commission, 1936
J.R.S.	*Journal of Roman Studies*
Lakeland Rambler	Year Book of the Ramblers' Association
P.N.C.	*Place-Names of Cumberland*, 3 vols, 1950-2
P.N.W.	*Place-Names of Westmorland*, 2 vols, 1967
T.A.S.L.C.	*Transactions of the Archaeological Society of Lancashire and Cheshire*
T.C.W.A.A.L.S.	*Transactions of the Cumberland and Westmorland Association for the Advancement of Literature and Science*
T.D.G.A.N.H.S.	*Transactions of the Dumfries and Galloway Antiquarian and Natural History Society*

Introduction, pages 11-14

For the influence of historic events on the folklore of Cumbria see the Introduction to the *Place-Names of Cumberland*, Pt. III, xiii ff. and the *Place-Names of Westmorland*, Pt. I, xvii ff.

For the quotation on NEOLITHIC PASSAGE GRAVES AND SYMBOLS see Evan Hadingham, *Ancient Carvings in Britain*, 1974, 7, 79; also Jill Purce, *The Mystic Spiral*, 1974, Plates 55 and 56. CAESARIAN

151

RULERS OF RHEGED: R. Cunliff-Shaw, *The Men of the North,* (no date given) Ch. III, W. G. Collingwood, *CW2,* XX, 1920, 53ff. N. K. Chadwick, *Celt and Saxon,* 1963, see Index under Urien and Owain. ARTHURIAN LORE. all references are given in the Notes to the chapter on *History in Legend* elsewhere in the book where relevant.

For PROFESSOR JACKSON on Britons and Saxons see his *Language and History in Early Britain,* 1953, 245.

1 *The Supernatural,* pages 15-36

GIANTS: Kirksanton; W. G. Collingwood, *The Lake Counties,* 1933, 69. Ravenstonedale: *I.H.M.W.,* 1936. xxxv-xxxvi. Penrith: the Giant's Thumb, Grave and Caves at Isis Parlis: W. G. Collingwood, *CW2,* XX, 1920, 53ff. XXIX, 1929, 47-8; A. J. Heelis, *CW2,* XIV, 1914, 337ff. W. S. Calverley, *Early Sculptured Crosses,* 1899, 240-6. For *The Dream of Rhonabwy,* see Gwyn and Thos. Jones, (translators) *The Mabinogion,* Everyman 1974, 137-152, and Collingwood, *CW2.* XX, 1920, 63-4. For the place name *kemp = cempa,*: A. H. Smith (ed) *English Place Name Elements,* 1956, XXV, Pt. One, 88. Calverley, 245. Dunmail: Roger of Wendover, H. O. Coxe (ed.) *Flores Historiarum,* 1841, I, 398. F. M. Stenton, *Anglo-Saxon England,* 1947, 355, 364. Collingwood, *The Lake Counties,* 1933, 159. Dunmail's cairn: J. M. Ewbank (ed.) *Antiquary on Horseback,* 1963, a selection from the Journal of Rev. Thos. Machell, 1691-2, 144-6. M. E. C. Walcott, *A Guide to the . . . Lakes,* 1860, 115. Hugh Heard: Ewbank, 126-7. J. Clarke, *A Survey of the Lakes,* 1869, 136-7.

FIENDS' FELL or CROSS FELL:: P,N,C, I, 243, III, IXXIX; Altar on, J. P. White, *Lays and Legend of the English Lakes,* 1873, 203.

The DEVIL: Near Gosforth: C. A. Parker, *The Gosforth District* 1904, 39. Kirkby Lonsdale: Devil's Bridge, Devil's Punch Bowl and Neck Collar; A. Pearson, *Annals of Kirkby Lonsdale,* 1930, Ch. VII. Apron String etc. ibid. 140 cit. Rev. J. Hutton's *Tour to Ingleborough.* See also, *P.N.W.* I, xlviii, 55 and 193 under *Skirtful Crags.*

WITCHES: Casterton: Bull Pot of the Witches, *P.N.W.* I. xlviii, 28. Langdale: E. M. Ward, *Days in Lakeland,* 1948, 74-5. Margaret Teasdale: Collingwood, *The Lake Counties,* 1933, 133. Hand of Glory: W. Henderson, *Folklore of the Northern Counties,* 1967, 239, 241. Mary Baines of Tebay: G. Findler, *Legends of the Lake*

Counties, 1967, 16-17.

THE WIZARD MICHAEL SCOT: Holland's trans. of Camden's *Britannia,* passage cited by F. Grainger and W. G. Collingwood (eds) in *Records of Holm Cultram,* 1929, *C.W.(R.S.)* Vol. VII, 135. Satchells cited by J. Wood Brown in *The Life and Legend of Michael Scot,* 1897, 176-7 221-2 and see Grainger and Collingwood, 135, Re James Jackson's *Diary,* 1650-83 see F. Grainger, (ed.) *CW2,* 1921, XXI, 103-4. Cit. from E. Sandford (c.1675) see his *Antiquities,* 31. Hutchinson, II, 329. Bolton Old Church, Collingwood, *Lake Counties,* 110. Carrock Fell McIntyre, 207. Scot's modern reputation, Lynn Thorndike, *Michael Scott,* 1965, p. I. Re Criffel, A. Craig Gibson, *Popular Rhymes . . . in Cumberland,* 1861, 10-11.

ELVES AND FAIRIES: *P.N.C.* 209, 418, 439. *P.N.W.* I, xlv, 175. Bewcastle: Rev. H. J. Bulkley, *CWI,* VIII, Pt. II, 227. For further elf howe lore see E. S. Hartland, *Science of Fairy Tales,* 1925, L. Spence, *Fairy Tradition in Britain,* 1948 H. Ellis, *The Road to Hel,* The cult of Freyr: Ellis, IIIf. Elf-shot Cattle: Thos. Davidson, *Antiquity,* No. 119, Sept. 1956, 149. Henderson, 185, *Bandamanna Saga*: ibid, 186N. Bishop Nicolson *Diary, CW2,* IV, 58. Letter from the Bishop: W. Hutchinson, *History of Cumberland,* I, 82. (1794-97) Reprint 1974. Lamplugh Register: C.M.L. Bouch, *People and Prelates of the Lake Counties,* 1948, 242. 'Fairy' place names: Fairy Steps, Arnside: W. R. Mitchell, *Around Morecambe Bay,* 1966, 38. Fairy Hole, Haverbrack, *I.H.M.W.* 104 b. The Fairies' Kettle, and the Fairy Kirk, near Caldbeck: R. Millward and A. Robinson, *The Lake District.* 1970, 39. Hutchinson, II, 388-9. Eveling and Ravenglass: W. G. Collingwood *CW2XXIV,* 256 ff. Caerthannoc: Rev. H. Mc.Clean in 1911 recorded a story about Caerthannoc in *CW2,* XII, 145 told by Rev Isaac Todd (born Wreay, 1797) Fairy horsemen: At Lanercost: Rev. H. H. Bulkley recorded in 1885 people still living had heard fairy riders. *CWI,* VIII, Pt. ii, 227. Fairy tobacco pipes: Mrs Hodgson, *On some Surviving Fairies, CW2,* 1900, 116 ff. Fairy Butter: ibid, 116 and L. Spence, *Fairy Tradition in Britain,* 1948, 187-8. Picts, Pixies, see R. Kirk, Introduction to the 1933 edition, of *The Secret Commonwealth of Elves and Fairies Draugr*: Ellis, *Road to Hel.* 90 f.

PHANTOMS: Calgarth Hall: Clarke. 134. A. C. Gibson, *Folk*

Speech of Cumberland, 1969, 54 ff. J. P. White, 177. Collingwood, *Lake Counties,* 27. The Crier of Claife: White, 26-7, Gabriel Hounds: Henderson, 129f.

BOGGLES: At Cappleside Hall, Beetham: Henderson, 275-6. J. F. Curwen, *CW2,* XII, 104-5. Ogier the Dane's fight with a *capalus,* R. S. Loomis, (ed.) *Arthurian Literature of the Middle Ages,* 15, 68.

HOBS: White 160 ff.

DOBBIE STONES: J. H. Palmer, *Historic Farmhouses in Westmorland,* 1944 edn. 18, 92.

JINNIE GREENTEETH: Author's personal recollection from about 1908. Pearson, 75-6.

T'TAGGY BELL: Editor of *Cumbria* 1970, Sept. 293.

2 *History in Legend,* pages 37-56

ARTHURIAN LORE: K. H. Jackson, *The Gododdin,* 19, Rheged: P.N.W. Introduction, xxxv-vi. Chadwick, *Celt and Saxon,* 19, 159, 329-30. Camlann: L. Alcock, *Arthur's Britain,* 1974, see Index. *Antiquity,* IX, (1935) 289; Jackson, *Modern Philology,* XLIII 56. Ravenglass and Eveling: Collingwood, *CW2,* XXIV, 256. Modron: Loomis (ed.) *Arthurian Literature of the Middle Ages,* see Index. Faery motif, ibid, 66. Caer Siddi: ibid, 15, n.6. and p.16. John Denton: Collingwood, *CW2,* XXIV, 256. Sir Thos. Malory, *Le Morte d'Arthur,* 1912, Macmillan, 151-2. The Lady of the Fountain: Jones (trans.) *The Mabinogion,* 155ff. Birkby: *P.N.C.* Pt. II, 424, Collingwood, *CW2,* XXIV, 259. Ravenglass bridge: Collingwood, *CW2,* XXIX, 39-40. Lanercost Chronicle: J. Stevenson (ed) *The Lanercost Chronicle,* Maitland and Bannatyne Club, 1839, 23. Blencathra Legend: Calverley, 247. Arthur's *burh: P.N.C.* 50. Rev. J. Wilson, *CW2,* III, 248. John Denton, *Estates and Families in Cumberland.* 1887 (Tract Series of C&W. Arch Soc.) 99, 100. Henry I's Charter confirmed, *Charter Roll,* 8 Ed. II, m.8. William of Malmesbury, *De Gestis Pontificuim,* N.E.S.A. Hamilton (ed.) Rolls Series, 208-9. British Carlisle: Chadwick (ed.) *Early British Church,* 19, 72-3. Glastonbury and Arthur: Alcock, 76, and see R. F. Treharne, *The Glastonbury Legends,* 1967. Yvain: Loomis, *Arthurian Literature,* 14, 112. Pendragon Castle: *Chancery Warrants.* I. 291 The Cliffords and Prince Llewelyn: Sir M. Powicke, *The Thirteenth Century,* 1953, 428, n.i. Llewelyn's crown: ibid, 429, n.3. Minstrels: Loomis, 59. Uther and Geoffrey

of Monmouth: E. K. Chambers, *Arthur of Britain,* 1927, 31-5.
Uther's date: Loomis, 14, 112. Rev. J. Wharton *CW2,* I, 408.
Lammerside Castle: Th. Pennant, *Tour from Downing to Alston,*
1801, cit. H. S. Cowper, *CW2,* IV, 90, Giant Carrado: Loomis,
337. Round Tables: Studies in Memory of *A. Kingsley Porter*
(Harvard University Press) 1939, 92-3. Arthur's Round Table, nr.
Penrith: C. W. Dymond, *CWI,* XI, Pt. I, 200ff. Wm. Atkinson,
CWI, VI, Pt. ii, 444ff. Stukely's sketch f.p. 450. Dr. Gerhard
Bersu, *CW2* XL, 169ff. Re Leland: *P.N.W,* Pt. Two, 205.
Hutchinson on the Round Table, *Excursion to the Lakes,* 1776, 90.
Castle Rock of St. John: *P.N.C.* Pt. II, 316, n. I. Hutchinson,
History of Cumberland, II, note cit. from *Excursion to the Lakes.*
Norse *borg* there: W. G. Collingwood, *CW2,* XVI, 224f. but see
P.N.C, Pt I, 253, n.2. *Awntyres off Arthure:* Loomis, 526 ff. Court
Thorn: Hutchinson, *History of Cumberland,* I, 504. Tarn Wadling:
Laikibrait, R. C. Cox, *Folklore,* Vol. 85, Summer, 1974. LV
(1944) 2ff. *The Marriage of Sir Gawaine,* Hutchinson, *History of
Cumberland,* I, 491-3. F. J. Childe (ed.) *English and Scottish Popular
Ballads,* 1956 edn., 288-96, 297-300. Castle Hewin: Hutchinson,
I, 492-3. II, 263-4. T. H. B. Graham, *CW2,* IX, 209-12.
Cumbria, J. Grimshaw, *Cumbria,* 1973, November, 447-9. Penrith:
Millward and Robinson, 147 and Plate 9. See also Collingwood,
CW2, XX, 53ff. *Avowynge of King Arthur P.N.C.,* Introduction
Pt. III, xix. Loomis, *Arthur. Literature,* see index. Wolsty Castle:
Collingwood, *Lake Counties,* Gazeteer, 355.
VORTIGERN: For *Sainct Johnes Chappel,* see *P.N.C.* Pt. II, 293.
Nennius's legend of Vortigern: A. W. Wade-Evans, (ed.) *History of
the Britons* by Nennius, 1938, 62-6. Red Dragon, ibid, 65, n.i.
Guasmoric: Wade-Evans, *CW2,* XLIX, 219-20. R. G.
Collingwood, *CW2,* XXVIII, 110-112. Prof. E. Birley, *CW2,*
LI, 38-9. *The Antiquary,* XLI, 409f. Llyyfenydd and Urien: A. H.
A. Hogg, *Antiquity* No. 80, Dec. 1946, 210-11. *P.N.W.* Pt. One,
XXXIV-V, and n.5. R. G. Collingwood *CW2,* XXXIII, 209-12.
CARLISLE: Luguvalium: *P.N.C.* Pt. I, 40-2. Birley *CW2,* XLIX,
219 cit. Jackson, *Journal of Roman Studies,* xxxviii, 1948, 54-58.
C. Squire, *Mythology of the British Islands,* 1905, 42, 276, 409 and
see *Lug,* in the index of Loomis, *Arthurian Literature.*
WINSTER: P. N. W. Pt. One xxxv, 14-15.
GWENDOLAU AND RHYDDERCH: Carwinley: *P.N.C.,* Pt. I, 52-3,

51 n.i. and Pt. III, xviii. For *Arfderryd,* ibid, Pt. I 51-2 under Arthuret. See also, Pt. III xviii. H. Barnes, *CW2,* VIII 236 ff. also A. O. H. Jarman, in Loomis, *Arthurian Literature,* 21-3. Myrddin and Kentigern: Loomis 20-30, Barnes, 242, 243. Rhun: *Chadwick, Early British Church,* 72ff. 114-5. Rienmelth; Chadwick, *Celt and Saxon,* 41-2.

OSWY & RIEMMELTH

HORN OF EGREMONT: Parker, 18 and McIntyre *Lakeland* ... 232-33. Other heraldic legends: McIntyre, 233-35.

SIR THOMAS BROUGHTON: F. R. C. Hutton, *CWI,* 1901 188-9.

PRINCESS OF FINSTHWAITE: H. S. Cowper, *Hawkshead,* 1899, 252-4; Lydia F. Thomas, *Forgotten Princess, Lakeland Rambler,* No. 23, 1962, 30-2. Taylors and Backhouses: J. F. Curwen, ed. *Records of Kendale,* III, 1926, 225, 262. Also information from Mr & Mrs Kellett, Chapman House, Finsthwaite, communicated to author September 1975.

3 *Legends of the Saints,* pages 57-70

For a recent general discussion of early legends and sources by scholars see M. W. Bailey and R. P. C. Hanson (eds) *Christianity in Britain, 300-700 A.D.*

ST NINIAN: Bede on St Nynia: J. McQueen, *St Nynia,* 1961, 1-2., and see *W. D. Simpson, New Light on St. Ninian Archaologia Aeliana,* XXIII,1945, 78ff. and Dr. W.L.,Levison,'*An 8th C. Poem' Antiquity,* XIV, 1940, 287ff. For a discussion of the sources for the *Lives* of St. Ninian see N. K. Chadwick the *Trans. of the Dumfries ... Antiquarian Society,* XXVII, (1950) 3rd Ser. Brougham: W. D. Simpson, *St Ninian,* 1940, see index. C. M. L. Bouch: *CW2,* LV, 108ff. The church of Ninekirks, Brougham: Bouch, *CW2,* L, 80; Brougham and Isis Parlis Caves: A. J. Heelis, *CW2,* III, 353f., XIV, 339-341. Brampton and St. Ninian: Simpson, St. Ninian, 82-8 Salway, *Frontier People,* 150. F. G. Simpson and I. A. Richmond, The Old Church, Brampton, *CW2,* XXXVI, 178-182. Martindale: *P.N.W.* II, 215., St Martin's Church, Bowness on Windermere, re the date of the font see N. Pevsner, *Buildings of Cumberland and Westmorland,* 1967, 228.

ST PATRICK: For discussion re sources: Hanson, *St Patrick,* 1968, the *mansio* at Ravenglass: R. G. Collingwood, *CW2,* XXIV, 249 M. C. Fair, XXV, 374-5. R. G. Collingwood, ibid, XXVIII, 357 ff. Re-occupation in Middle Ages, ibid 366. Salway, 125-6. Patrick's Ash, Aspatria, *CPN*, Pt. II, 262. W. G. Collingwood, *CW2*, XXIII 245, W. T. McIntyre, *CW2*, XLIV, 4-5. Chapel at Heysham: J. BuLocke *Trans. Arch. Soc. of Lancs and Cheshire*, 1967. E. Baines, *History of Lancashire*, 1870. II, 529.

ST KENTIGERN: A. P. Forbes (ed.) *Lives of St Ninian and St Kentigern*, Historians of Scotland Series, 1874, Vol V. Discussion of sources: Chadwick (ed.) *Early British Church*, 1958, Chapter on *Kentigern* by Prof. K. H. Jackson. Morken: also re Mockerkin, McIntyre Lakeland, 227, see C. A. Raleigh Radford, *Hoddom* in *Antiquity*, 107, Sept. 1953, 154. Crosthwaite and Church: F. C. Eeles, *The Parish Church of St Kentigern*, 1953. See pp. 1, 2 re date of church. Early village at Crosthwaite: Rev. Canon Rawnsley, *CW2*, IV, 254ff. Well: McIntyre, *CW2*, XLIV, 8, Collingwood *Lake District History*, 38, Churches and wells dedicated to the saint: For those mentioned in the text see Index, P.N.C. Pt III. Also T. Lee, *CW1*, VI, Pt. II, 328. Wells: McIntyre, *CW2*, XLIV, 1ff. but see M. C. Fair, ibid, LII, 189ff. For the legends illustrated by the Keswick School coat of arms: A. P. Forbes, 83ff.

ST CONSTANTINE: Forbes, 95, 366. Hutchinson, *History of Cumberland*, I, 160-3. Chadwick, ed. *Early British Church*, 320. Clericatus: Chadwick, *Celt and Saxon*, 332.

ST CUTHBERT: B. Colgrave (ed.) *Two Lives of St Cuthbert*, 1940. Traditional paintings: ibid 31-2. Wanderings with relics in Cumbria: Rev. T. Lees, *CW1*, II, 14ff. D. Scott, *CW2*, XXII, 443, and footnote. T. H. B. Graham, ibid, XXV, 12-14. For 'Helly Well and St Cuthbert's Stone near Waverbridge: Francis Grainger, *CW2* XII. 432.

ST HERBERT: Thos. Lees, *CWI*, Pt. II 1882,338.

ST BEGA: *The Life and Miracles of St Bega the Virgin*, 12th Century, in The *Register of the Priory of St Bees*, Surtees Soc. Vol. 126, 1915. Her arm ring: L. A. S. Butler, *CW2*, LXVI, 1966, 92ff. C. E. Last, *CW2* LII, 55ff. D. R. Fyson, *CW2*, LVII, 30-2. Custom re oaths on arm rings: Stenton, 251. Theft of St Bega's arm ring: Butler, 104. Edmund Sandford's account of St Bega: *Antiquities and Families in Cumberland* c. 1675. 9f. St Bega's well: C. A. Parker, *CW2*, IX, 1909, 113-14.

4 *Symbols, Myths and Folklore from Pagan and Christian Monuments,*
pages 71-85

CUPS, RINGS AND SPIRALS: Illustration of the Maughanby Stone:
Rev. Canon Thornley, *CW2*, II, facing p. 381. Glassonby stone
illustration: ibid, f.p. 382. New Grange illustration: Jill Purce, *The
Mystic Spiral*, 1974, PL. 56. Old Parks: Chancellor Ferguson,
CWI, XIII Pt. II, PL. VIII. Long Meg, ibid, PL. IX, Photograph
of tatooed Maori, Purce, PL. 47. Article on Spirals: W. F. J.
Knight, *Antiquity*, No. 24, December 1932, *Maze Symbolism, and
the Trojan Game*, 445ff. A Thom. *Megalithic Lunar Observatories,*
1971.

THE MAZE AND THE TROJAN GAME: Troys: Purce 29. The Solway
Walls of Troy: R. S. Ferguson, *CW1*, VII, 1884, 69 ff. W. H.
Mounsey, *Notes and Queries*, Series II, V, 211. W. H. Matthews,
Mazes and Labyrinths, Chs. X and XI. Julian's Bower: W. J.
Knight, *Antiquity*, 453. Re *Iulus* as the name for a maze Knight
cites Matthews, 71, 78, 90, 173, 230. For Julian's Bower see also
Nicolson and Burn, I, 278. Re Mazes and Maidens: W. J. Knight,
450, n 30. Hopscotch: Purce, p.115, Par 66 and illustration, p.
114, No. 66. Iceland folklore: *PNW* pt.II 223

PLACE NAMES WITH *KIRK* : See Introduction, *P.N.W.* Pt. One, xxxi.
Kirksanton: *P.N.C.* II, 415-16. Sunken Kirk, ibid, 417, J.
Ecleston, *CWI*, I, Pt. 3, 281. Hutchinson, History of Cumberland,
I. 554 and citation from Gough's Camden, Addns. in footnote.
Kirkstone Pass: Ewbank, 148. Stave churches: E. O. G.
Turville-Petre, *Myth and Religion of the North*, 1964, III, Pl.6.
Cairn: *PNW*. Pt. Two, 223, Hoff Lunn: ibid, Pt. One, xlv. Pt.
Two, 97, 99, also Pt. One xxvi, xxxiv. xlv.

LONG MEG: Prof. F. Haverfield on *Cotton Iulius F.VI* in the British
Library, being notes by Reginald Bainbrigg of Appleby and Cam-
den on Cumbrian antiquities written before 1623. *CW2*, XI. 343
ff. For Long Meg see 361-2. Origin of name: E. C. Brewer,
Dictionary of Phrase and Fable, 13th edn. 523. O. G. S. Crawford,
Long Meg, Antiquity No. 31, Sept. 1934, pp. 328-9 with
Stukeley's sketch on 16 August 1725, f.p. 336 and cf. Crawford's
photograph, 20 May 1934, PL.II. For Druid folklore see
Professor Stuart Piggott, *The Druids*, Thames and Hudson, 1968.
Vol 63 in *Ancient Peoples and Places* series. For dates of circles see
I.H.M.W. xxxi.

THE 'COUNTLESS STONES' MYTH: S. P. Menefee, *Folklore*, 86, Autumn/Winter, 1975, 146-66. J. Baron, *All About the Eng. Lakes,* under *Long Meg. P.N.C.* III, 238.

WHITHORN STONE WITH CROSS AND SPIRAL: W. G. Collingwood, *Northumbrian Crosses,* 1927, p. 3. No. 8.

PAGAN AND CHRISTIAN SYMBOLISM OF ANGLIAN AND NORSE CROSSES: Professor Toynbee: see Bailey and Hanson (eds.) 180ff. Dearham cross: W.S. Calverley, *Early Sculptured Crosses,* 1899. 124-5. Gosforth cross: Calverley, 139ff. Collingwood, *Northumbrian Crosses,* see Index C. A. Parker and W. G. Collingwood, *CW2* XVII, 99ff.

CHURCH LEGENDS: Bolton Old Church: Collingwood, *Lake Counties,* 1933, 110. Crosby Garrett, E. Bogg, *Wandering in the Border Country,* 1898, Pt. II, 114. Kirkby Lonsdale: Pearson, 137. 'Lost' church of St Michael, Addingham: Bogg, Pt. II, 65. C. J. Gordon, *CW2* XIV, 328 ff.

CHURCH BELLS: Great Salkeld; G. Fidler, *Legends of the Lake Counties* 1967. 54. Blawith: J. Baron, *All About the English Lakes,* 1925. Boot in Eskdale: St Catherine's Well and Bell Hill, Hutchinson, *History,* I, 580 but see *C.P.N.* I, 117 Bowness on Solway: Arthur Mee, *The Lake Counties,* 33.

ROBIN THE DEVIL: Ewbank: 88. Nicolson and Burn, I, 142, 181, J. Clarke, *Survey* 134, C. Nicholson, *Annals of Kendal,* 55 n.3. J. F. Curwen, *Kirkbie-Kendall,* re Mr John Broadbent 247. Re the sword, 252. Legend 252., also see *Cumbria,* August 1955, 184-5 re, Belle Halliwell recorder.

5 *The Lucks of Cumbria,* pages 86-94

THE LUCK OF EDENHALL: For a detailed description and discussion of its origins and artistic merit see Llewelyn Jewitt in *The Reliquary,* Vol. 19, 1879. *The Victoria and Albert Museum,* Pamphlet 6371 gives further details about the Luck. For the vessel as a sacramental chalice see A. J. Heelis, *CW2,* III, 354. XIV, 341, note. The earliest ' printed account of the Luck appeared in the *Gentleman's Magazine,* August 1791. Re the Goblet of the Eight Priests: *V. & A. Museum* pamphlet, p.3. The Luck of Ballafletcher: Hartland, *Science of Fairy Tales,* 158, n.i. On Christianizing pagan vessels, ibid, 156-7. Norse idea of luck: H. F. Ellis, 130-35. Berg women: Hartland, 158, i. Re Mr Davidson and Miss Graham of Edenhall:

The information was a personal communication by Miss Graham and Mrs Towler of Edenhall given to me in 1975.

THE LUCK OF MUNCASTER: C. A. Parker, *The Gosforth District,* 1904, 203-4. Colonel Sherwood, curator of Muncaster Castle reported by G. R. Phillips on the Luck in *Cumbria,* April 1973, p. 34.

THE LUCK OF BURRELL GREEN: Llewelyn Jewitt, *Art Magazine,* Dec. 1879. J. Lamb of Burrell Green, *CWI,* XV, Pt. I 136. (1898) D. Scott, *CW2,* XIII, 1913, 124. Mr and Mrs S. Armstrong tenants at Burrell Green – personal communication to G. R. Phillips recorded in *Cumbria,* April 1973, 34. John Burrell: *PNC,* I, 231, 238. Celtic platter or *Graal*: Loomis, 280-2, Drinking horns: Ibid, 287, 2,294.

THE LUCK OF WORKINGTON: Details from a letter kindly sent by Mr R. W. D. Wetenhall of the Curwen Estates, Workington.

THE LUCK OF HARESCEUGH CASTLE: Personal communication to G. R. Phillips from Mr Hugh C. Little of Station House, Steeton, Keighley, recorded in *Cumbria,* April 1973, 32. Norse place name: *C.P.N.* Pt. I, 216, 227.

THE LUCK OF NETHER HARESCEUGH: G. R. Phillips in *Cumbria,* April, 1973, 33 citing Colonel T. Fetherstonehaugh from his *Our Cumberland Village,* 1925.

THE LUCK OF RYDAL HALL: Recorded by C. Roy Hudleston in *CW2,* LXIV, 289-90 citing the will of Sir William Fleming of 'Rydall' in 1736. See portrait, f.p. 264.

RETURN OF LUCK MONEY: Personal communication to me by Mr R. Thompson, Lickbarrow Cottage, Windermere in 1975. Also see Henderson, 119. F. W. Horrobin at Lazonby, *Cumbria,* Sept. 1972, 321.

SALT LEFT ON A PLATE FOR LUCK: B. L. Thompson (ed.) *Some Westmorland Villages,* Recorded by member of Bampton Women's Institute, p.8.

6 *Nature Lore,* pages 95-107
TREES: Dryad: Brewer, 247. Rowan and Gaels: Chas. Squire, *Mythology of the British Islands,* 1905, 219, 410. Making butter come: H. S. Cowper, *CWI,* XIV, 1897, 375. Yew Tree: The dead-light: Personal communication to me by my husband in 1973. Yew branch and the dead-light: H. J. Bulkley, *CWI,* VIII, Pt. II,

1886, 230 Protection against evil: Ibid, 230. Tree and well dressing: Collingwood, *CWI*, XIII Pt. II, 1895, 405. Hazel Lore: Water divining: Brewer 392. In graves: Calverley, 118-9. 122 n. Hazel worm, R. S. Ferguson in last paragraph of note to the article by G. S. Stephens and W. S. Calverley, in *CWI*, VI, Pt. II, 367. Hazel staves round Norse Law courts: Turville-Petre, 238. Kentigern: Calverley, *Early Sculptured Crosses*, II. Hawthorn: Court thorn near Hesket: *CPN*, 123, 200, 202-3, xix. Hutchinson, History, I. 504, Mee, 102. At Anthorn: *CPN*, 123, 292. Collingwood, *CW2*,XXIX, 1929, 212-13.

TRADITIONS RE TREES AND PLANTS: Hartshorn Tree: G. C. Williamson, *Lady Anne Clifford*, 1922, 9, 10, 11. Sir Jas. Clarke's *Journal*, 1731, ed. by W. A. J. Prevost, *CW2*, LXI, (1961) 219. Nicolson and Burn, I, 399. F. H. Parker, *CW2*, X 9. The Capon Tree: *CPN*, 67. Hutchinson, I, 129, Lore recorded by H. Penfold: *CW2*, V, 129ff. Holly: Brewer, 411. House Leek: Personal communication by Mrs Berry of Heathwaite, Windermere in 1970. Devil's fruit: Ibid. and see Henderson, 96.

WEATHER LORE: Skiddaw: McIntyre, 225. A Craig Gibson, *Popular Rhymes*, II St Bees, McIntyre, 226. Falls on the Kent and Bela: Nicolson and Burn, I, 208. St Swithin: Brewer, 868-9. Remaining lore from author's childhood recollections, c. 1910.

ANIMAL TRADITIONS: The Last Wolf: at Humphrey Head. Poem in Stockdale's *Annals of Cartmel*, cited in full in Mrs Jerome Mercier's *The Last Wolf*, printed in Grange over Sands, no date given. Ulpha near Grange: *PNW*, I 76. Last Wolf of Scotland: McIntyre, Lakeland and Borders, 178. Wotobank: ibid, 177-8. Ulpha Old Hall: J Lofthouse, *Off to the Lakes*, 1949, 39.

The Last Boar: Kentmere: Ewbank (ed.) 90. At Kirkby Stephen: Bruce Thompson (ed.) 86, F. B. Chancellor, *Around Eden*, 1954, 33. Bogg Pt. II, 113.

IMMORTAL FISH: White, 224, The Shepherd Lord: E. Robinson, *Wordsworthshire*, 1911, 57. Wordsworth's poem re the fish: *The Song of Brougham Castle*.

BIRDS: Magpies and crows: Personal communication by M. and N. Herd of Hutton Roof nr. K. Lonsdale, c. 1909. Crows on fallow: T. Makin of Kent recalling a jingle heard when living in W. Cumberland. *Cumbria.* 1973, Jan. 586. Cocks: on churches: S. Heath, *Romance of Symbolism*, 1909, 53, 156. A *crouse* cock: A.

Craig Gibson, *Folk Speech of Cumberland*, 1880, 171. At Bampton: Bruce Thompson, 8. Pent Cuckoo: E. J. Field, *The Myth of the Pent Cuckoo*, 1913, reviewed in *Folklore*, XXV, 1914, 390-1. *CPN*, 349.

7 *Calendar Lore*, pages 108-128

NEW YEAR'S DAY: First Footing: Henderson. Customs re water: Informant a Caldbeck girl. Recorded in 1900 — Mrs Hodgson of Newby Grange in *CW2*, I, 118.

CANDLEMAS DAY: Re Catholic ceremony: Brewer, 138. J. C. Robinson of Staveley, weather prophecies in *Cumbria*, 1973, July, 265. W. G. Collingwood's anecdotes: *The Lake Counties*, 144. That about Bishop Gibson illustrates the scholarship of a Bampton countryman but also north country wit and humour. For this see pp. 143-4. Mrs Little: *Chronicles of Patterdale*, 1961, 66.

ST VALENTINE'S DAY: Origin of custôm of sending a romantic greeting; Ditchfield, 53 and J. Jackson, *Cumbria*, 1957, February, 391. Anne Stables card (of Howtown) Pooley Bridge, ibid, 389-90.

SHROVE TUESDAY: Brewer 68. For a list of where *barring out* took place see the Opies, 239, 240n. At Bromfield (c. 1764) Hutchinson, II, 312n. At Patterdale (1892-8) Little, 61-2. I personally recall that several spring games began on this day around Kirkby Lonsdale and Kendal.

APRIL NODDY AND MAY GESLING: Brewer 38. April Noddy was kept up in my home until around 1922. May Gesling was not regularly remembered.

EASTER: Tid, Mid and Miseray: The rhyme was taught to me around 1910 by May Howson of Hutton Roof when I was a child. See, Bulkley, *CWI*, VIII Pt. 2, 232.

CARLIN' SUNDAY: *CWI*, VIII, Pt 2. 232. *CW2*, XV, 115, foot-note citing Brand, *Popular Antiquities*, 56-8.

MOTHERING SUNDAY: Opies, 242. Simnel Cake: Obviously a *simnell* has long been associated with Mothering Sunday, see Herricks poem — 'I'll to thee a simnell bring, Gainst thou goest a mothering.' But the tea table at Easter always held a simnel cake in my own family, back to my grandmothers time. The custom continues in my daughter's household.

MAUNDY THURSDAY: Jolly Boys: Dr E. M. Wilson, *CW2*,

XXXVIII, 165-6. ibid. in *Folklore*, 49, (1938) 36ff. Mrs Ruth Atkinson reports her husband (born in Westmorland at Skelsmergh) was a Jolly Boy. On Maundy Thursday he and others gathered tins, dragged them through the village and sang, 'Trot earins, trot on, Good Friday ta morn'. *Cumbria*, 1956, June, 99.

GOOD FRIDAY: Fig Sue: Soak 1lb of figs, chop and boil in a little water. Add milk and chopped bread with sugar and salt. Boil 10 mins. Add beer or ale if liked. Serve on thick round of bread. M. A. Wood, Helsington Kendal, in *Cumbria* 1957, April, 31. But see *Cumbria*, 1957, July, 139.

EASTER: New clothes for: J. O'Connor, *Memories of Old Kendal*, 1961. *Folklore* XI (1929) 284. Rolling pace eggs: O'Connor, 150. Grandy Needles: ibid 150.Dumping eggs: Venetia Newall, *An Egg at Easter*, 1971, 347, citing *The Cumberland Evening News*, 25 April, 1957. Wordsworth pace eggs: Newall, 281. Foster eggs: ibid, 362 with illustrations on facing page.

Easter football: Morris Marples, *Cumbria*, 1970, March, 647-8. McIntyre, 213. Jolly Boy's Play: One version given – Pearson, 187, ff. Peter Jackson records Jonty Wilson in *Cumbria*, 1970, December. 466. J. H. Palmer records Mr C. Clarke of Hollins Farm, nr. Kendal in *Historic Farmhouses in Westmorland*, 1944, 66. Easter Ledge Pudding: Mrs Scott re Easter May Giant pudding, *Cumbria* 1954, June 102. Recipe: Lakeland Cookery, Dalesman Publishing Co., Clapham. p.7.

FIRE FESTIVALS: Miss Senhouse recorded John Shepherd of Gosforth, *CW2*, II, 82. Shaking Bottle Sundays: Personal communication from Miss Graham in 1974. Brand, *Popular Antiquities*, cited by C. E. Golland in *CW2*, XV, 115, footnote. Bottle rite at Greystoke: E. A. Askew, informed the Bishop of Barrow in Furness re the Well ceremony at Greystoke; recorded in footnote, *CW2* III, 21. At Isis Parlis Caves, Golland, *CW2*, XV, 115ff. and footnotes.

MAY DAY: At Melmerby: E. Kingsdale, Cumbria 1955, May, 64. At Wetheral: M. Kirkpatrick, *The Story of Wetheral*, 1959, 17. At Temple Sowerby, Bogg, 121.

OAK BOB DAY: *Local Chronology*, 1865, 97. E. M. Wilson in *CW2*, XXXVIII, 165 footnote. At Windermere: Barring out in 1883, Old Boys Association, compilers *History of Windermere Grammar School*, 1936. Horses decked with oak leaves in 1888 –

Westmorland Gazette, May, 1938 in 50 Years Ago column. Mrs E. Brocklebank, born in Ambleside records Yak Bob Day there around 1910 in *Cumbria,* January 1973, 585. Re hitting with nettles in Kirkby Lonsdale around 1910 – personal recollection.
RUSH BEARING: At Burton in Kendale: Ewbank, 46. *Cumbria,* 1955, June, 86. E. C. Dawson's letter, 1956, March, 436-7. Clara Boyle, Ambleside Letter, 1956, May, 64. At Warcop Hall; in the Eden valley: Cyril Harrington, 1956, November, 270. Boyle, *The Rushbearing, Cumbria,* 1961, Sept. 233. E. F. Rawnsley, *Rushbearing in Grasmere and Ambleside,* 1953 (pamphlet).
MIDSUMMER: Bonfires in Cumberland see Dr Lyttleton, Bishop of Carlisle in *Antiquities of Cornwall,* London, 1769, 135n. For Machel, see Ewbank, 46. Bonfire fare at Crook c.1940 author's personal recollection. At Wetheral: Midsummer Wakes – M. Kirkpatrick 31. Around Keswick: The *Bel-tin,* Thos. Pennant, *A Tour* . . . (1801) cited by Hutchinson, *History,* II, 162.
HALLOWE'EN: T. Carrick of Wigton. Folklore XI (1929).
FIRE CEREMONIES AND TRADITIONS: Twelfth Night at Brough: *Carrying the Holly Tree,* W. H. Hewitson, Hone's *Table Book,* Vol 2, (1827-28) 26f. With illustration. For different versions see, F. B. Chancellor, *Around Eden,* 1954, 47-8. The Need Fire in Cumberland: Mr and Mrs Hodgson of Newby Grange recorded its use in 1865 or 66 informer an inhabitant of Scaleby in 1901, CW2. I, 118 and W. Wilson records its use in 1887 'in the dales': *Former Social Life in Cumberland and Westmorland, T.CWAALS,* XII, 1887, 85. Unquenched hearth fires, Coniston: T. Ellwood of Torver, *The Landnama Book re Folklore of Cumberland & Westmorland. CWI,* XII, Pt. II, 1893, 287-290, *CWI,* XIV, 376. Tullithwaite Hall: Underbarrow: Bruce Thompson, 206. H. S. Cowper, *Hawkshead Folklore, CWI,* XIV, Pt. 2, 376.
HARVEST FESTIVALS: The Luck Sheaf: T. Carrick of Wigton, Folklore XI, 1929. Kern Suppers: Bruce Thompson, 32. See also, Brown, *Round Carlisle Cross,* 1924, 4th series, 48-9.
CHRISTMAS: Recipe for Sweet Pie from the author's Family Recipe book of 1894. That for Kendal Wigs has the name of Miss Edmondson attached. The Christmas play: from information by the Author's mother around 1920. Dancing and singing at Christmas in 1917, author's personal recollection.

8 *From Birth to Burial,* pages 129-138

BIRTH: Jack O'Connor, 66-8. 'In the clouts', Bishop Nicolson, *Diaries,* 1712, *CW2,* IV, 58. Rum butter a births and christenings; Rollinson 54. Buttered sops; an egg and salt: J. Budworth, *Diary,* 1810, 30. Bruce Thompson, 9. Calendar rhyme: Author's personal recollection from c. 1908.

DIVINATION THROUGH GAMES AND RHYMES: Re love and marriage: Pippin, Paradise: McIntyre 227. Apple peel etc: Personal recollection from c. 1910. Skipping rhymes, idem. Sneezing: Editor, *Cumbria,* 1974, May, 63.

BIDDEN WEDDINGS: Brown, *Round Carlisle Cross* 1951, 141-2. Rollinson, 57-8 Pearson, 177 Sneckin' Oopt'yate: McIntyre, 211-12. Rubbing with pease straw: P. H. Ditchfield, 195-6. Henderson, 41. Clay daubin: Brown, 140 and see R. W. Brunskill, *Vernacular Architecture of the Lake Counties,* 1974, 110, (d), 113. Bridewains: Brown, 142-3 Corn laitin': Hutchinson, I, 553.

ILLNESS CHARMS AND DEATH: Pearson, 205. Bulkley, *CWI,* VIII, 226 and see *CW2,* XV, 115, and footnote 3. Telling the bees: Personal recollection to author. Brown, 131-2. *CWI,* VIII, pt. 2, 229. The passing bell: Pearson, 179. Brown, 131.

FUNERALS: Bidders: W. Dodd ed., *Edenhall,* 1974. Informant J. Mallinson about 1910. O'Connor, 69. Killington: Pearson, 29 also Nicolson and Burn, I, 264. Corpse Roads: Rollinson 59-60. Parker, 98. Pearson, 29, Nicolson and Burn, I, 264.

9 *Traditional life,* pages 139-150

Memories of a fell-farm: The author's recollections c.1908.

SHEEP FARMING: Herdwick sheep: E. M.Ward, *Days in Lakeland,* 77ff. Rollinson: 82-3. Sheep scoring numerals: Ellwood, *CWI,* III, Pt. ii, 381ff. Shepherds' meets: Ward, 102-4. Sheep dogs: ibid 101-2.

HAND KNITTING: Rollinson, 55. Marie Hartley and Joan Ingleby, *Old Hand Knitters of the Dales,* 1969. In Kendal. 52 ff. Knitting Sheathes, ibid 77-80 and photos, Pls. V-VIII, Also Parker, *Knitting Sticks CW2,* XVII, 88f. Striking the loop: Bruce Thompson, 56. Bulls at bay: Mrs Hodgson, *CW2,* I, 118. Clever lass of Dent. Hartley & Ingilby, 58. Betty Yewdale: ibid, 60-1.

PACK-HORSES AND INNS: Frank Graham, *Old Inns and Taverns of Lakeland,* 1967, 14. A Lakeland breakfast, 1842, Ibid, 14.

Drunken Duck tradition: ibid, 15.

PEDLARS AND TAILORS: Old Mary: Mrs Brocklebank, Millom, Letter to *Cumbria,* December 1970, 492. Visiting tailors: Alfred Langstrath, *Bassenthwaite's Tommy Whipcat,* recording J. W. Holt's personal recollections as a visiting tailor in Cumberland before the First World War. *Cumbria,* 1958, August, 169-170. Martha Chamley and Mrs Proctor: personal recollections by the author in the early years of the century.

HUNTING: Re John Peel: The Centenary Programme Oct. 1954, 4-17. Song *'D'ye ken John Peel'* ibid., 13 and see Brown, 206ff. Oil painting by Graves: this can be seen by appointment in the Board Room of Redmaynes (Tailors) in Wigton. This information kindly supplied by J. J. Bagley. See article (anonymous) on Peel in *Cumbria,* September 1972, 330-1, 334.

COCK FIGHTING: Rollinson, 141-7.

WRESTLING: Ibid, 161-4.

FAIRS: Hiring: Bouch and Jones, *Lake Counties,* 337-8. Rollinson, 160-1. Egremont Crab Fair: Local Pamphlet, 1974.

Bibliography

The books and articles listed below are the main printed sources of the Lake District folklore. Reference to the other works which contain isolated stories or traditions will be found in the Notes. *The Bibliography and Topography of Cumberland and Westmorland,* (1968) compiled by H. H. Hodgson is also most useful.

L. Alcock, *Arthur's Britain,* 1974

M. L. Armitt, *Rydal,* 1916

W. Atkinson, 'Earthworks near Eamont Bridge' *CWI,* VI, Pt. ii, 444-455

M. W. Bailey and R. A. C. Hanson, eds. *Christianity in Britain, 300-700, A.D.,* 1968

E. Baines, *History of Lancashire,* II, 1870

H. Baines, 'On the Battle of Ardderyd,' *CW2,* VIII, 1908, 236-246

J. Baron, *All About the English Lakes,* 1925

G. Bersu, 'King Arthur's Round Table', *CW2,* XL, 1940, 169-206

E. Birley, 'Roman Fort at Old Carlisle', *CW2,* LI, 1952, 16-39. 'Some Roman Place-names in Cumbria', *CW2,* XLIX, 1950, 219-20

Bishop of Barrow-in-Furness, 'Bishop Nicolson's Diaries', *CW2,* IV, 1904, 1-70

E. Bogg, *Wandering in the Border Country and Lakeland,* 1898

C. M. L. Bouch, *People and Prelates of the Lake Counties,* 1948. 'Ninekirks, Brougham', *CW2,* L, 1951, 80-90. 'A Dark Age Coin Hoard from Ninekirks', *CW2,* LV, 1956, 108-111

C. M. L. Bouch and G. P. Jones, *The Lake Counties,* 1961

F. C. Brewer, *Dictionary of Phrase and Fable,* 13th edition

B. J. Wood Brown, *Life and Legends of Michael Scot,* 1897

J. W. Brown, *Round Carlisle Cross,* 1951

R. W. Brunskill, *Vernacular Architecture of the Lake Counties,* 1974

W. S. Calverley, *Early Sculptured Crosses,* 1899

T. W. Carrick, 'Scraps of English Folklore', *Folklore*, XL, 1929, 278-290

N. K. Chadwick, *Celt and Saxon*, 1963. ed. *Studies in the Early British Church*, 1958. 'Preliminary Study of the Sources for the Life of St Ninian', *T.D.G.A.N.H.S.* XXVII, 1950.

E. K. Chambers, *Arthur of Britain*, 1927

F. B. Chancellor, *Around Eden*, 1954

F. J. Childe, ed., 'The Marriage of Gawain' in *English and Scottish Popular Ballads*, 1956

J. Clarke, *A Survey of the Lakes*, 1789

B. Colgrave ed., *Two Lives of St Cuthbert*, 1940

R. G. Collingwood, 'The Last Years of Roman Cumberland', *CW2*, XXIV, 1924, 247-55. 'Old Carlisle', *CW2*, XXVIII, 1928, 110-12. 'Prehistoric Settlements at Crosby Ravensworth', *CW2*, XXXIII 1933, 208-12

W. G. Collingwood, *Lake District History*, 1925. *Northumbrian Crosses*, 1927. *The Lake Counties*, 1933. 'The Castle Rock of St John's Vale', *CW2*, XVI, 1916, 224-8. 'The Giant's Thumb', *CW2*, XX, 1920, 53-65. 'An Inventory of Cumberland', *CW2*, XXIII, 1923, 206-276. 'Manx Names in Cumberland', *CW1*, XIII, Pt.ii, 1895, 403/14. 'Ravenglass in Ancient Deeds', *CW2*, XXIX, 1929, 39-48. 'Who was King Eveling of Ravenglass?', *CW2*, XXIV, 1924, 256-259

H. S. Cowper, *Hawkshead*, 1899. 'Hawkshead Folklore', *CW1*, XIV, Pt. ii, 1897, 371-89.

H. O. Coxe, 'Lammerside Castle', *CW2*, IV, 1904, 85-91

H. O. Coxe, See Roger of Wendover

R. C. Coxe, 'Tarn Wadling and Laikibrait', *Folklore*, LXXXV, Summer 1974, 128-131

O. G. S. Crawford, 'Long Meg', *Antiquity*, No. 31, Sept. 1934, 328-9

R. Cunliffe-Shaw, *Men of the North*, 1973

J. F. Curwen, *Kirkbie-Kendall*, 1903. ed. *Records of Kendale*, Vol. III, 1926. 'Cappleside Hall', *CW2*, XII, 1912, 104-6

Thomas Davidson, 'Elf-shot Cattle', *Antiquity*, No. 19, Sept. 1956, 149-155

J. Denton, *Estates and Families . . . in Cumberland*, 1887, *CW*(TS)

P. H. Ditchfield, *Old English Customs*, 1896

W. Dodd, *Edenhall*, 1974

C. W. Dymond, 'Mayburgh and King Arthur's Round Table', *CWI*, XI, pt. i, 187-219

J. Eccleston, 'Ancient remains at Kirksanton', *CWI*, Pt. III, 1883, 278/81

F. C. Eeles, *The Parish Church of St Kentigern*, 1953

H. R. Ellis, *The Road to Hel*, 1913

T. Ellwood, 'The Landnama Book and the Folklore of Cumberland and Westmorland', *CWI*, XII, Pt. ii, 1893, 283-311

J. M. Ewbank, ed., *Antiquary on Horseback*, the Journal of the Rev. T. Machell (1691-2) 1963

M. C. Fair, 'Ancient Ford on the River Mite', *CW2*, XXIX, 1929, 259-264. 'Holy Wells of Cumberland', *CW2*, LII, 1952, 189-91

R. S. Ferguson, 'A Labyrinth on Rockcliff Marsh', *CWI*, VII, 1884, 69-73

J. E. Field, *The Myth of the Pent Cuckoo*, 1913

G. Findler, *Legends of the Lake Counties*, 1967

A. P. Forbes, ed. Lives of St Ninian and St Patrick, Historians of Scotland series, Vol. 5, 1874

D. R. Fyson, 'St Bega's Bracelet', *CW2* LVII (1958) 30-2

A. C. Gibson, *Folk Speech of Cumberland*, 1869

C. J. Gordon, 'A Submerged Church in the River Eden', *CW2*, XIX, 1919, 328-36

F. Graham, *Old Inns and Taverns of Lakeland*, 1967

T. H. B. Graham, 'Extinct Cumberland Castles,' *CW2*, IX, 1909, 209-12. 'Patron Saints of the Diocese of Carlisle', *CW2*, XXV, 1-27

F. Grainger and W. G. Collingwood, eds. *Records of Holmd Cultram*, 1929, *CW*(RS), Vol. VII.

F. Grainger, 'The Hellinwell at St Cuthbert's Stone', *CW2*, XII, 1912, 432. 'James Jackson's Diary', *CW2*, XXI, 1921, 103-4

W. Green, *Tourist's New Guide to the Lakes*, 2 vols, 1819

J. Grimshawe, 'A lost Castle', *Cumbria*, 1973, November, 447-9

Evan Hadingham, *Ancient Carvings in Britain*, 1975

R. S. P. C. Hanson, *St Patrick*, 1968

E. S. Hartland, *The Science of Fairy Tales*, 1925

M. Hartley & J. Ingilby, *The Old Hand Knitters of the Dales*, 1969

F. Haverfield, 'Notes on Bainbrigg and Camden' (Cotton Julius f.VI), *CW2*, XI, 1911, 343-78

S. Heath, *The Romance of Symbolism*, 1909

C. Headlam, ed., *The Three Northern Counties of Britain*, 1939

A. J. Heelis, 'The Caves of Isis Parlis', *CW2*, XIV, 1914, 337-42. 'Ninekirks', *CW2*, III, 1903, 353-65

W. Henderson, *Folklore of the Northern Counties*, 1866; Reprint 1967

Mrs Hodgson, 'On Some Surviving Fairies', *CW2*, I 1901. 116-18

H. W. Hodgson, ed., *Bibliography of the History and Topography of Cumberland and Westmorland*, 1968

A. H. A. Hogg, 'Llwyfenydd', *Antiquity*, Vol 80, Dec. 1946, 210-11

W. Hone, *Table Book*, Vol. 2, 1827-8

F. W. Horrabin, 'Among the Sheep Men', *Cumbria*, September 1972, 321

C. Roy Hudleston, 'The Fleming Family', *CW2*, LXIV 1964, 264-305. 'The Luck of the Scarsgill', *CW2*, LXVIII, 1968, 195-6

R. W. Hunt, ed., *Studies in Medieval History presented to F. M. Powicke*, 1948

W. Hutchinson, *History of Cumberland*, 2 vols, 1794-7, Reprint 1974

F. R. C. Hutton, 'Witherslack . . . Manor', *CWI*, 1901, 188-9

K. H. Jackson, *The Gododdin*, 1969. *The Language and History of Early Britain*, 1953. 'On some Romano-British Placenames', *J.R.S.*, XXXVIII, 1948, 54-8

J. Jackson, 'Good morrow to my Valentine', *Cumbria*, 1957, February, 389-91

P. Jackson, 'Jonty Wilson's Christmas', *Cumbria*, 1970, Dec., 466-68

A. O. H. Jarman, 'The Welsh Myrddin Poems', A. Loomis, ed. *Arthurian Literature of the Middle Ages*, 21-3

G. & T. Jones, tr., *The Mabinogion*, Everyman, 1974

R. Kirk, *The Secret Commonwealth of Fairies*, 1692; reprint 1933

M. Kirkpatrick, *The Story of Wetheral*, 1959

W. F. J. Knight, 'Maze Symbolism and the Trojan Game', *Antiquity*, No. 24, Dec. 1932, 445-458

Kingsley-Porter, see W. R. W. Koehler, ed., *Medieval Studies in Memory of Kingsley Porter*, 1939

J. Lamb, 'The Luck of Burrell Green', *CWI*, XV, Pt i 1897, 136-8

C. E. Last, 'St. Bega and Her Bracelet', *CW2*, LII, 1953, 55-66

T. Lees, 'St Kentigern and his dedications in Cumberland', *CWI*, VI, pt. ii 1883, 328-337

W. L. Levison, 'An 8th-century poem on St Ninian', *Antiquity*, XIV, 1940, 280-91

E. A. Little, *Chronicles of Patterdale*, 1961

J. Lofthouse, *Off to the Lakes*, 1949

R. S. Loomis, ed., *Arthurian Literature of the Middle Ages*, 1954

T. Machell, see Ewbank

Sir T. Malory, *Morte d'Arthur*, Macmillan, 1912

Wm. of Malmesbury, *De Gestis Pontificum*, ed. N.E.S.A. Hamilton, Rolls Series, 52.

M. Marples, 'Old English Football at Workington', *Cumbria*, 1970, March, 647-8

W. H. M. Matthews, *Mazes and Labyrinths*, 1922

W. T. McIntyre, *Lakeland and the Borders*, 1948. 'List of the Holy Wells of Cumberland', *CW2*, XLIV, 1944, 1/15

H. McClean, 'Caerthannoc', *CW2*, XII, 1912, 143-45.

J. MacQueen, *Saint Nynia*, 1961

S. P. Menefee, 'The Countless Stones: A Final Reckoning', *Folklore*, Vol. 86. Autumn/Winter 1975

W. R. Mitchell, *Around Morecambe Bay*, 1966

Nennius, See Wade-Evans

Venetia Newall, *An Egg at Easter*, 1971

C. Nicholson, *Annals of Kendal*, 1861

Bishop Nicolson, *Diaries*, edited by the Bishop of Barrow-in-Furness, *CW2*, III, 1904, 1-70

J. Nicolson and R. Burn, History of Cumberland, 2 vols, 1777

J. O'Connor, *Memories of Old Kendal*, 1961

I. & P. Opie, *The Lore and Language of School-children*, 1959

J. H. Palmer, *Historic Farm Houses in Westmorland*, 1944

C. A. Parker, *The Gosforth District*, 1904. 'Some Medieval Crosses', *CW2*, IX, 1909, 78-119

C. A. Parker & W. G. Collingwood, 'Gosforth Cross Reconsidered', *CW2*, XVII, 1917, 99-113

A. Pearson, *Annals of Kirkby Lonsdale*, 1930

T. Pennant, *A Tour from Downing St to Alston Moor*, 1801

G. R. Phillips, 'Quest for the Cumbrian Lucks', *Cumbria*, 1973, April, 30-4

Stuart Piggott, *The Druids*, Pelican 1975. 'Mummers Plays from . . . Cumberland and the Isle of Man', *Folklore*, XL, (1929)

Sir. M. Powicke, *The Thirteenth Century*, 1953

F. M. Powicke, See R. W. Hunt

Rev Canon Rawnsley, 'Early Man at Crosthwaite', *CW2*, IV, 1904, 254-6

E. F. Rawnsley, *Rushbearing in Grasmere and Ambleside*, pamphlet 1953

I. A. Richmond, 'Old Church, Brampton', *CW2*, XXXVI, 172-82

Ritson, *Life of King Arthur*, 1825

E. Robinson, *Wordsworthshire*, 1911

W. Rollinson, *Life and Tradition in the Lake District*, 1974

P. Salway, *Frontier People of Northern Britain*, 1965

E. Sandford, *Antiquities and Families in . . . Cumberland*, c.1675, *CW*(TS) No. 4, 1890

D. Scott, 'The Luck of Burrell Green,' *CW2*, XIII, 1913, 124-7. 'Milburn Church', *CW2*, XXII, 1922, 442-6

W. D. Simpson, *St. Ninian*, 1940. 'New Light on St Ninian', *A.A.*, Vol. 23, 1945, 78ff.

A. H. Smith, *English Place Name Elements*, 1956

R. R. Sowerby, *Kirkby Stephen*, 1948

L. Spence, *The Fairy Tradition in Britain*, 1948

C. Squire, *Mythology of the British Islands*, 1905

F. M. Stenton, *Anglo-Saxon England*, 1947

J. Stevenson, ed., *The Lanercost Chronicle*, Maitland and Bannatyne Club, 1839

A. Thom, *Megalithic Lunar Observatories*, 1971

Lydia F. Thomas, 'Forgotten Princess', *Lakeland Rambler*, No. 23, 1962, 30-2

B. L. Thompson, ed., *Some Westmorland Villages*, 1957

Lynn Thorndike, *Michael Scot*, 1965

R. F. Treharne, *The Glastonbury Legends*, 1967

E. O. G. Turville-Petre, *Myth and Religion of the North*, 1964

A. Wade-Evans, ed., *History of the Britons*, by Nennius, 1938. 'Guasmoric', *CW2*, XLIX, 1949, 219-20

M. E. C. Walcott, *Guide to the Mountains, Lakes and North-West England*, 1860

E. M. Ward, *Days in Lakeland,* 1948

T. West, *Guide to the Lakes,* 1778

J. Wharton, 'Pendragon Castle', *CW2,* II, 1902, 408

J. P. White, *Lays and Legends of the English Lakes,* 1873

G. C. Williamson, *Lady Anne Clifford,* 1922

E. M. Wilson, 'Folk Traditions in Westmorland', *Journal of the Folklore Institute,* Indiana, 1965, Vol. 2, 276-93. Some Extinct Kendal Customs,' *CW2,* XXXVIII, 1938, 164-179

J. Wilson & Sir E. T. Bewley, 'Bewley Castle' *CW2,* III, 1903, 240-61

James Wilson, 'The Medieval Name of Old Carlisle', *The Antiquary,* XLI, Jan-Dec. 1905, 409 – II.

P. A. Wilson, 'St Ninian and Candida Casa', *T.D.N.H.S.,* 1964, 156-185

W. Wilson, 'Former Social Life in Cumberland & Westmorland', *T.C.W.A.A.L.S.,* XII, 1887, 67-86

Old Boys Association, *History of Windermere Grammar School,* 1936

Museums

Barrow-in-Furness: Ramsden Square. Lake District bygones.
Brampton: Banks near the Roman Wall. Cumbrian Folk Art.
Carlisle: Tullie House, Regional Collections.
Grasmere: Dove Cottage, Wordsworth's early home furnished as during his occupation.
The Wordsworth Museum, near Dove Cottage, illustrates the rural life of Wordsworth's period.
Hawkshead: The Court House Folk Museum.
Kendal: Abbot Hall Museum of Lakeland Life and Industry.
Kendal Borough Museum: Many Kendal bygones.
Millom: St Georges Road. Folk Museum.

Full particulars about the above museums are printed in *Lakescene*, which is published each month.

Two albums of period photography provide illustrations of folk life in the Lake District. They are:
Irvine Hunt, *The Lakeland Pedlar*, 1974
Irvine Hunt, *Fenty's Album*, 1975

Daphne Foskett, *John Harden of Brathay Hall, 1772-1847*, 1974, is illustrated by John Harden's own sketches and paintings which 'conjure up vividly the life of that bygone age' as lived not only by a 'normal happy family of the upper middle class in the Lake District' but by country people, scullery maids, dairy maids, a quill winder, the village 'dame' school mistress and her pupils, the smith in his 'smiddy' and others.

Index of Tale Types

Folktales have been classified and named on an international system based on their plots, devised by Antti Aarne and Stith Thompson in *The Types of the Folktale*, 1961; numbers from this system are preceded by the letters AT. Local legends have been partially classified by R. Th. Christiansen in *The Migratory Legends*, 1958; his numbers are preceded by ML. Brackets round an entry signify that the story from the Lake District only partially resembles its international prototype.

Motif Index

A motif is an element that occurs in the plot of one or several folktales (e.g. 'cruel stepmother', which occurs in 'Cinderella', 'Snow White', etc.) They have been classified thematically in Stith Thompson's *Motif Index of Folk Literature*, 1966; the numbers below are taken from this, and from E. Baughman's *Type and Motif Index of the Folktales of England and North America*, 1966.

General Index